M/9

POSTSCRIPT ON *BEOWULF*

POSTSCRIPT ON
BEOWULF

BY

S. O. ANDREW, M.A.

NEW YORK / RUSSELL & RUSSELL

FIRST PUBLISHED IN 1948
REISSUED, 1969, BY RUSSELL & RUSSELL
A DIVISION OF ATHENEUM PUBLISHERS, INC.
WITH PERMISSION OF CAMBRIDGE UNIVERSITY PRESS
L. C. CATALOG CARD NO: 70-77668
PRINTED IN THE UNITED STATES OF AMERICA

CONTENTS

.PREFACE

This book, as its title implies, is a sequel to my *Syntax and Style in Old English*. The main object of that work was to determine the syntax of various sentence-forms in prose; the evidence of verse was indeed not ignored, but it was largely confined to showing that there was a *prima facie* case for believing tha the usage of verse, generally speaking, agreed with that of prose. It became clear, however, from the reviews that some of those who accepted the conclusions of the book in regard to prose idiom considered the evidence for verse dubious or at least insufficient, and I determined to examine that evidence more thoroughly. My first idea was to make a complete survey of the extant OE verse, but I soon discovered that this would involve the investigation of many preliminary problems (text, date, authorship, affinity) demanding an expenditure of time and space which I could not give. I therefore decided to limit my enquiry to *Beowulf*; this, the greatest in every sense of the OE poetic remains, is by its mere length its own best commentary, and any well-founded conclusions about it cannot fail to be of general importance.

The subject-matter of *Syntax and Style* (now out of print) is covered by the first five chapters of this book, though not always in the same order; a detailed statement of the problems dealt with will be found in the Introduction. Following suggestions by two friendly reviewers of *SS*, I have now given much more space to the examination of the co-ordinate clause, both asyndetic and other, and have also discussed certain stylistic features of the poem, e.g. (in Cap. vi) apposition, expletive *ðær*, parenthesis, and (in Cap. viii) the several kinds of 'transition' clause; Cap. vii deals with problems of the Parts of Speech.

A closer scrutiny of the *Beowulf* editions has led to my making some surprising discoveries, one of which by way of example I may mention here. Though all the four modern editions admit the subordination of a temporal clause when it follows the principal sentence, not one of them does so when the clause precedes the principal sentence. I have not been able to discover the origin of this curious superstition, but some of its unfortunate consequences in one kind of clause are pointed out in Cap. II, 9.

I am well aware of the great debt which OE scholarship owes to Sievers, but further study has confirmed me in the opinion expressed in my *OE Alliterative Measure*, that the accepted metrical classification (that of Sievers) suffers from a fatal flaw, namely, the assumption that any part of speech except nouns could be stressed or unstressed at pleasure; and I am now convinced that this assumption was the logical consequence of Sievers' self-imposed rule limiting postponed alliteration to A types. I would draw the reader's special attention to Chapters IX–XI, in which this subject is discussed; since collation fails us, for obvious reasons, in the textual criticism of *Beowulf*, a valid metrical criterion is an instrument which can ill be spared. The chapters mentioned are intended to take the place of my *OE Alliterative Measure*, which is also out of print.

Beowulf is a work of mature literary art; it will be seen that I think better of it in this respect than most of its editors. It is true that the style of the poem has its particular conventions; judged by modern standards of taste, it is overloaded with nouns and appositions, but that was part of the poet's inheritance and is no more to be counted against him than the fixed epithets and similar conventions of Greek epic are to be counted against Homer. Other supposed characteristics of *Beowulf*, however, e.g. the fragmentation caused by so-called paratactic sentences, are merely the result of modern mispunctuation and do not belong to the original; they form the subject, directly or indirectly, of Chapters II–V of this book.

In a final chapter I deal with problems arising out of scribal error and seek to formulate some of the general principles without which emendation of the *Beowulf* text can be little more than a 'guessing game'.

S. O. A.

January 1948

POSTSCRIPT ON *BEOWULF*

CHAPTER I

INTRODUCTORY

The three kinds of word-order in OE prose may be conveniently exemplified by a sentence in which both subject and object are pronouns:

(1) *Common order*, usual in principal sentences: Hi hine gebundon mid bæstenum rapum.

(2) *Conjunctive order*, the regular form after conjunctions and relatives: Ða hi hine mid bæstenum rapum gebundon.

(3) *Demonstrative order*, found in principal sentences of which the headword is a demonstrative adverb: Ða gebundon hi hine mid bæstenum rapum.

It will be observed that the sentences show characteristic differences in the positions of the pronouns. In (1) the pronouns usually precede the verb and in any case are not separated from it; in (2) they stand together immediately after the conjunction and may be widely separated from the verb, which normally comes at the end; in (3) they stand together immediately after the verb. The order of the pronouns among themselves is also governed by rule, the usual precedence being subject, direct object, indirect object, as in He hit me ageaf.

In *Beowulf*, as in prose, common and conjunctive order are frequent, and the pronouns are subject to the same rules both of position and precedence, as the following examples will show:

Common order: 292 ic eow wisige, 372 Ic hine cuðe, 1392 Ic hit ðe gehate, 1873 him wæs bega wen; inversion was normal in negative sentences and commands, e.g. 1322 Ne frin ðu æfter sælum, and it sometimes occurs in affirmative sentences with a stressed verb, e.g. 471 Sende ic Wylfingum maðmas.

Conjunctive order: 539 ða wit on sund reon, 1472 siððan he hine gegyred hæfde, 1625 ðara ðe he him mid hæfde, 2448 ond he him helpe ne mæg gefremman; sometimes the common order of the principal sentence is retained in the clause, as in ModE, e.g. 1095 Ða hie getruwedon frioðuwære. Only in 932 ðæt ic ænigra me, and 2157 ðæt ic his ærest ðe est gesægde, are the pronouns separated from each other (see 117).

Demonstrative order: of this there are over fifty instances with *ða* in *Beowulf*, e.g. 3058 Ða wæs gesyne ðæt se sið ne ðah, 1600 Ða com non dæges. Some of these might be subordinate clauses, as in prose, if *ða* were construed as the conjunction, and it is in fact generally agreed that the place of the principal *ða*-sentence with a stressed verb is usually taken in the poem by the forms *Com ða* (when the subject is a noun) and *He ða* (when it is a pronoun); the modern editors, however, make all the *ða com* sentences principal, as they do the similar *ðonne*-sentences.

We shall try in Chapter II to solve two main problems, (1) whether forms with conjunctive order, e.g. 1274 ða he hean gewat, 853 ðær him hel onfeng, are possible principal sentences, as the editors assume, and (2) whether forms like Ða com non dæges are always principal sentences, as the editors also assume. In Chapter III we shall deal with other kinds of adverbial clause and with some noun-clauses.

The pronoun *se ðæt* may be either demonstrative or relative. In prose, when the pronoun is the headword in a sentence with conjunctive order, it is always the relative. Such sentences are frequent in *Beowulf* and many of them, e.g. 1466 ðæt he ær gespræc, are rightly punctuated by editors as relative clauses, but many others are made principal sentences in which the pronoun is taken as the demonstrative. Is there any rational ground for this discrimination? The nominative *se*, when followed immediately by the verb, may in prose be the demonstrative, but only if it is the antecedent; the four editors, however, make it the demonstrative in *Beowulf* in every place where it stands next to the verb, whether it is the antecedent or not. Is this a proper construction? We shall discuss these two and other related problems in Chapter III.

In the *com ða* sentence-form the subject is often unexpressed if it is the same as that of the context. Does this justify the assumption that the subject-pronoun could be omitted in *any* kind of sentence, even when the subject changes? The problem, which is usually different for principal and subordinate sentences, will be discussed in Chapters v and vi.

Some general observations may here be made on the claim sometimes put forward that there is a 'psychological element' in language which entitles a poet to a special freedom in the use of it, especially as regards word-order. Few will dispute this, unless it means that the poet is above all law and can do anything he likes. It does not seem unreasonable, however, to ask for a definition of the term 'psychological' by which it can be brought to account. Analogy is generally admitted to be a psychological element in the making of language, and, as such, it may rightly be called in to justify an unusual construction. Since, however, it is a defined term, any claim made for it can be tested. For instance, some editors defend the omission of *ðæt* before any noun-clause by the analogy of the *cwæð* construction in 199 'cwæð he guðcyning... secean wolde' and elsewhere; the conjunction, however, is never omitted after this verb if the subject of the following clause is different from that of *cwæð* itself, as it is in all the first-mentioned clauses. The test therefore fails and there is no analogy (see further 34). Should we be any better off with the undefined 'psychological' element? Or is this a mere name for something unknown, like the phlogiston of the older chemistry?

There is another assumption, much more widely applied, which calls for a preliminary word of warning. Words like *ða, ær, nu* are ambiguous in their written form; each one of them is really a homograph and represents two different parts of speech, an adverb and a conjunction, which must always have been distinguished in the spoken language as stressed and unstressed. It is, no doubt, this identity of written form which has produced the illusion that the *adverbs* could be stressed or unstressed at pleasure. One example, not more astonishing than others, may be given. There are twenty-eight instances in *a* verses of the *ða wæs* sentence-form, in which *ða* is admitted by everybody to be the adverb; fourteen of them, e.g. ðá wæs on búrgum, scan as regular A types, and the other fourteen, e.g. ðá wæs Hróðgàre, as regular Dx types. Yet Sievers and his followers, while admitting the stress on *ða* in the fourteen A types, deny it in all the fourteen Dx types, which they therefore classify as B or C. This simple example must suffice for the present; the problem of stress will be fully discussed in Chapter IX, and that of metrical classification in Chapters X and XI.

CHAPTER II

SENTENCES INTRODUCED BY *ÐA, ÐONNE, ÐÆR*

Numerals in heavier type, e.g. (43), refer to sections of this book; the letters *SS* followed by a numeral, e.g. (*SS* 69), refer to sections of my *Syntax and Style in OE*. The 'four editions' mentioned from time to time are those of Holthausen, Klaeber, Sedgefield and Wyatt-Chambers; these agree, with small variations, in the punctuation of the text, but for convenience of reference, passages are cited, in the first six chapters, as they appear in Klaeber's edition.

1. In prose, *ða*-sentences with conjunctive order, e.g. *ða ic ðæt geseah*, are (*SS* 10) unambiguously subordinate clauses. It will be well, before going further, to restate the evidence on which this rule was based, viz. that in OE texts which are close translations of Latin originals, e.g. *Bede* or Ælfric's *OT.*, the sentence-form mentioned is consistently used to render a Latin subordinate clause; the instances in *Bede*, some half-dozen altogether, in which a *ða*-sentence with conjunctive order renders a Latin principal sentence, are examined in *SS* 6 and there shown to be only apparent exceptions which admit of a different explanation. Since usage in the mature prose of Aelfric's *Homilies* agrees, the evidence is conclusive that the rule was as stated; is there any reason to suppose that the rule in poetry, and specifically in *Beowulf*, was different?

2. Before we attempt to answer this question, a remarkable circumstance must be mentioned. None of the four editions recognises the subordination of any kind of *ða*-clause except when it *follows* the principal sentence, as in

539   Hæfdon swurd nacod,   ða wit on sund reon:

no fewer than forty-six *ða*-clauses in *Beowulf* which thus follow the principal sentence are punctuated, quite correctly, as subordinate; when, however, any similar *ða*-clause precedes a principal sentence, it is invariably pointed, in all the editions, as itself a principal sentence. I have searched diligently but in vain for an explanation of this strange treatment (it goes back as least as far as Grein) and can only assume that it derives from some traditional theory of poetic syntax or style whose origin I cannot trace; the unanimity of the editors does not appear to admit of any other conclusion. I commend the problem to the reader's attention as one that ought to be cleared up (see further 9).

3. Let us now take a survey of the *ða*-sentences with conjunctive order which the modern editions punctuate as principal sentences; they are thirty-three in number and it will be convenient to consider them under several heads:

(i) where they stand next to sentences to which they are really subordinate:

83
                  ne wæs hit lenge ða gen
      þæt se ecghete...wæcnan scolde.
      Ða se ellengæst   earfoðlice
      þrage geþolode,   se þe in þystrum bad.

389
                  (Ða wið duru healle
      Wulfgar eode,)   word inne abead:

461
                ða hine Wedera cyn
      for herebrogan habban ne mihte.
      Ðanon he gesohte Suððena folc...:
      ða ic furðum weold folce Deniga
(there are two *ða*-clauses here)

518
              Ða hine on morgentid | holm up ætbær;
      ðonon he gesohte   swæsne eðel,

541
              No he wiht fram me
      fleotan meahte,...no ic fram him wolde.
      Ða wit ætsomne   on sæ wæron

579
      siðes werig.   Ða mec sæ oþbær,

728
      Geseah he in recede   rinca manige,
      swefan sibbegedriht...Ða his mod ahlog;

1095
      Ða hie getruwedon   on twa healfa
      fæste frioðuwære.   Fin Hengeste
                ...aðum benemde,

1274
              Ða he hean gewat...,
      mancynnes feond.   Ond his modor þa gyt
      gifre ond galgmod   gegan wolde...

1605
              Ða þæt sweord ongan...
      wigbil wanian;   þæt wæs wundra sum,...

1665
      Ofsloh ða æt þære sæcce...
      huses hyrdas.   Ða þæt hildebil
      forbarn brogdenmæl,

1698
              Ða se wisa spræc
      sunu Healfdenes   —swigedon ealle—:

2131   Ða se ðeoden mec   ðine life
            healsode hreohmod...;   he me mede gehet.
2312   Ða se gæst ongan   gledum spiwan,
            beorht hofu bærnan,   —bryneleoma stod
            eldum on andan;
2628   ne his mæges laf
            gewac æt wige;   þa se wyrm onfand,
2711   Ða sio wund ongon...
            swelan ond swellan;   he þæt sona onfand,
3060   Weard ær ofsloh
            feara sumne;   þa sio fæhð gewearð | gewrecen
3169   Ða ymbe hlæw riodan   hildediore,

4. Most of these *ða*-clauses are temporal, but a few, e.g. 83, are causal; in 461 both kinds are found qualifying the same principal verb 'gesohte'. The bracketed words in 389, which are the accepted emendation, cannot stand, since neither clause in the passage can be a principal sentence; see further 177. With 579, where the clause qualifies an adjective, cf. 1326 min eaxlgestealla ðonne we hafelan weredon, where it qualifies a noun. In 1274 'ond' is otiose in what can only be the principal sentence (16), and in 2629 Thorpe's emendation 'þæt' is generally accepted, though 'swa' is perhaps better; it was elsewhere (see 101) misread as *ða*. For 3169 see 14. The rest are straightforward, though 728 and 1665 require a special word of comment; as they stand, they can only be examples of the continuative use of *ða* (=whereupon) which is frequent (*SS* 38) in Alfredian translations and in Ælfric, and is certainly a Latinism. Is it a likely construction in an early poem like *Beowulf*? The idiom of the poet (31 *sqq.*) suggests *ðæt* (=so that) for *ða* in both places as an alternative.

For metrical objections to *ða* as adverb in many of the verses, see 150, 163.

5. (ii) Some instances are more complex because a sentence intervenes between the *ða*-clause and the principal sentence; the latter is usually of the *com ða* or the *he ða* type, as in

671   Ða he him of dyde   isernbyrnan,
                        ...sealde his hyrsted sweord,
            irena cyst,   ombihtþegne...
            ond gehealdan het   hildegeatwe.
            Gespræc þa se goda   gylpworda sum,

'When he had doffed his byrnie [and] given his sword to his man....'

1512   Ða se eorl ongeat
      þæt he in niðsele   nathwylcum wæs...
          ...;   fyrleoht geseah,
      blacne leoman,   beorhte scinan.
      Ongeat þa se goda   grundwyrgenne,

'When the earl perceived that he was in some hostile hall [and] saw the light of fire....'

2715   Ða se æðeling giong
      ðæt he gesæt on sesse;   seah on enta geweorc...
      Hyne ða mid handa   heorodreorigne
      ðegn gelafede

'When the atheling had gone to sit on the seat [and] looked on the giants' work....'

6. In the above examples the intervening sentence is an asyndetic co-ordinate clause (51); in others it may be a parenthesis, e.g.

229   Ða of wealle geseah   weard Scildinga
      beran ofer bolcan   beorhte randas,
      fyrdsearu fuslicu;   hine fyrwyt bræc
      modgehygdum,   hwæt þa men wæron.
      Gewat him þa to waroðe   wicge ridan,
662   Ða him Hroðgar gewat   mid his hæleþa gedryht...;
      wolde wigfruma   Wealhþeo secan,
      cwen to gebeddan.   Hæfde Kyningwuldor...
      seleweard aseted;

'When from the cliff the warden saw bright shields borne along the gangway (desire to know what men these were fretted his mind) then came he riding', etc. For other possible constructions, see further 61 and 70. The reader will observe that in all but one of the passages in these two sections there is a *ða-ða* correlation, a construction in which the first *ða*-sentence is normally (16) the subordinate one.

7. (iii) The five *ða ic gefrægn* sentences, viz.

74   Ða ic wide gefrægn   weorc gebannan...
      folcstede frætwan.   Him on fyrste gelomp...

2484 Ða ic on morgne gefrægn mæg oðerne
   billes ecgum on bonan stælan...;
   guðhelm toglad,

2694 Ða ic æt þearfe gefrægn þeodcyninges
   andlongne eorl ellen cyðan...
   Ne hedde he ðæs heafolan,

2752 Ða ic snude gefrægn sunu Wihstanes
   hyran heaðosiocum, hringnet beran...
   Geseah ða sigehreðig...

2771   Næs ðæs wyrmes ðær
   onsyn ænig, ac hyne ecg fornam.
   Ða ic on hlæwe gefrægn hord reafian,

'When (as the story tells) the task was laid on many a tribe', 'when on the morrow (as I heard the tale) one brother avenged the other', etc.

That these are subordinate clauses is proved by the occurrence of the formula in *b* verses, e.g. *Judith* 246, ða ic ædre gefrægn, where no scansion is possible unless *ða* is unstressed and therefore a conjunction. In all the five *Beowulf* verses a stressed *ða* is against metre (see 163). The corresponding principal sentence is *Gefrægn ic ða*, of which we have both positive and negative examples in

Jud. 7 Gefrægn ic ða Olofernus...winhatan wyrcan georne
Beo. 1011 Ne gefrægn ic ða mægðe maran weorode
   ymb hyra sincgyfan sel gebæran.

8. (iv) Sentences introduced by *ða ðær, ða ðæt*, e.g.

330   wæs se irenþreat
   wæpnum gewurþad. Ða ðær wlonc hæleð .
   oretmecgas æfter æþelum frægn:

'The mailed band was worthily weaponed when a proud man there asked them of their lineage.'

809 Ða þæt onfunde se ðe fela æror...
   fyrene gefremede...; wæs gehwæþer oðrum
   lifigende lað.

'When he who before had wrought malice on mankind found [that his body would not serve him], each to the other was hateful while he lived.'

1279 Com ða to Heorote, ðær Hring-dene
   geond ðæt sæld swæfun. Ða ðær sona wearð
   edhwyrft eorlum,

'when there was at once swift reversal for the earls.'

1596   þæt hig ðæs æðelinges   eft ne wendon,
        þæt he sigehreðig   secean come
        mærne þeoden;   þa ðæs monige gewearð,
        þæt hine seo brimwylf   abroten hæfde.

'since it seemed to many that the sea-wolf had destroyed him.'

These are usually taken as principal sentences in which *ða ðæt* and *ða ðær* are double demonstratives. There is no certain instance of a double demonstrative beginning a sentence in good prose, and no reason for assuming it in verse; all the exx. make good sense and good metre (129) if the *ða* is taken as a conjunction, as two editors do take it in 1596. As regards 1279 see the note on 728, 1665, in 4. The construction in 415 Ða me ðæt gelærdon leode mine, is obscure; 'ða ðæt me gelærdon' would be a good sub-ordinate clause, or 'me ðæt gelærdon' a good principal sentence of the *he ðæt* type (41), but *ða me ðæt* is neither one thing nor the other.

9. We may pause here for a few moments in order to assess the stylistic loss which the text of *Beowulf* suffers by the refusal of subordination, in all modern editions, to any *ða*-clause which precedes the principal sentence:

(i) All examples of *ða-ða* correlation (see 16) inevitably disappear, since in these the subordinate clause normally stands first. We are left instead with pairs of emphatic demonstrative sentences (then—then); sometimes there are three such sentences in sequence, as in 461 *sqq.* cited in 3 (then—thence—then).

(ii) All the 'transitions', both major and minor, which are so characteristic (103) of the poet's art, similarly disappear, e.g. (major) 229, 671, 809, 1095, 2312, 2752; (minor) 461, 518, 1605, 2711, all cited above (3–8).

(iii) In some places both idiom and sense are destroyed by attaching the clause to the wrong sentence, even when it is rightly construed as subordinate, as in

322   hringiren scir
        song in searwum,   ða hie to sele furðum
             ...gangan cwomon;...
        bugon ða to bence;

This is rendered 'the ring-iron sang as they approached the hall', but the *ða furðum* clause can only mean 'as soon as they reached the hall', and this makes no sense except when subordinate to 'bugon ða to bence' (see further 54); the full-stop should be after 'searwum', not after 'cwomon'.

2864   Ðæt la mæg secgan   se ðe wyle soð specan...
          ðæt he genunga   guðgewædu
          wraðe forwurpe,   ða hine wig beget.
          Nealles folccyning   fyrdgesteallum
          gylpan ðorfte;

'A truthful man may well say that he (your lord) recklessly threw away the war-gear'—when? Obviously, as we are told, whenever (*ðonne*) he gave it at the ale-drinking, not 'when war (still in the future) came'. Attach the *ða*-clause to the following sentence, and we have proof of the truth-speaker's statement: 'when war came, he found you to be cowards'.

10. Two of the reviews of *SS* sought to justify the *ða he geseah* form of principal sentence by citing *ASC* 853 'Ða ðy ilcan geare E. and H. gefuhton' or the like. In such sentences, which are not uncommon in OE prose, the reader will observe that the adverb *ða* is defined by an adverbial phrase of *time* coming immediately after. Should these opening words be followed by the demonstrative order which is the rule after *ða* itself or by the common order which is usual after an adverbial phrase? As we might expect, both orders were equally good usage, e.g.

(1) *Hom.* I.,450. 25. Ða on ðære ðriddan nihte geseah se bisceop...
    ASC 893. Ða sona æfter ðæm com Hæsten mid LXXX scipa...

(2) *Bede* 148. 32. Ða æfter Edwines slege S. Paulinus genom ða cwene.
    Matt. xx. 6. Ða embe ða endlyftan tide he uteode.
    ASC 895. Ða ðy ylcan geare onforan winter ða Ðeniscan tugon hira scipu up on Temese.

It is clear that such instances as those in (2) are a special class which constitute a real exception to the regular *ða*-construction. The analogy cannot, however, be extended from these to supposed principal sentences generally in which *ða* by itself is followed by common or conjunctive order.

In *Beowulf* neither of the (1) and (2) types illustrated above occurs at all. It is true that there is a superficial resemblance to (1) in 229 Đa of wealle geseah weard Scyldinga, and to (2) in 2484 Đa ic on morgne gefrægn mæg oðerne..., but in 229 the adverbial phrase is not one of time, and in 2484 the subject-pronoun is in the wrong place, separating *ða* from the adverbial phrase. We must conclude that the prose idiom in (2) gives no warrant for the supposed exceptions in *Beowulf*.

11. *The ða com form.* The sentence-form in which *ða* is immediately followed by a stressed verb is, in prose, ambivalent, that is, it may be either principal or subordinate; normally, it is a principal sentence in prose and indeed is one of the most common forms of it in all periods of Old English. In *Beowulf* there are only six examples of the *ða com* form, a number frequently exceeded in a single page of prose; they are

710	Đa com of more...Grendel gongan...;
	mynte se manscaða manna cynnes
	sumne besyrwan
1160	Gamen eft astah,
	beorhtode bencsweg...Đa cwom Wealhþeo forð
1600	Đa com non dæges. Næs ofgeafon
	hwate Scyldingas;
1644	Đa com in gan ealdor ðegna...
	Đa wæs be feaxe on flet boren
	Grendles heafod,
1802	Đa com beorht scacan
	scima ofer sceadwa; scaþan onetton,
2977	Let se hearda...entiscne helm
	brecan ofer bordweal; ða gebeah cyning...

In all the editions these are taken as principal sentences.

What are the objections to this construction? First, their extreme rarity, which is surely a warning sign of something exceptional; the *com ða* and *he ða* forms, which, as we shall see presently, take their place in *Beowulf*, number nearly a hundred. Secondly, in a *ða-ða* correlation, whereas in prose the *ða com* form is the usual principal sentence, it is never so in *Beowulf*, where the *com ða* form is invariable as in the exx. cited in 5; it will be observed that in the correlated pair, 1644 just above, *ða com* can only be the subordinate, not the principal, sentence. Moreover, if *ða com* is a principal sentence in 710 Ða com of more, why does it suddenly change to *com ða* in 720 com ða to recede, just below? Thirdly, unless we deny the adverb *ða* its stress, we have in four of the lines an unknown metrical type with four stresses, e.g. ðá cóm nón dǽges (see further 153). Fourthly, and most important, we have positive evidence that in *Beowulf* poetic convention rejected the demonstrative type of principal sentence with a stressed verb, for we have numerous instances (see 13) of the order Ymbeode ðá, and not one of Ðá ymbeode, though it is equally good metrically.

In all the first five examples a subordinate construction yields both good sense and good metre; for the sixth, 2977, see 31.

12. The sentence-forms in *Beowulf* that take the place of the prose form *þa com* as a principal sentence, are *com þa* and *he þa*, which occur eighty-five and eleven times respectively. In a *com þa* sentence the subject is frequently unexpressed where it is the same as that of the context; after a speech it may be the speaker or the person addressed. In

1920   Het þa up beran   æþelinga gestreon,

the right subject (Beowulf) has not been mentioned for nearly twenty lines and we should naturally, but wrongly, take it to be the same as in the sentence before, i.e. the harbour-ward; moreover, 'æþelinga gestreon' is a strange expression for Hrothgar's gift (1884 Hroðgares gifu, 1899 Hroðgares hordgestreon). The nominative 'æþeling' (=Beowulf, cf. 1815) must be the right reading.

If the subject of a *com þa* sentence is expressed, it is always a noun; the unique instance of a pronoun in 1563 He gefeng þa fetelhilt, has been defended as admitting of another interpretation, but if 'þa' is to be taken as the adverb the right order must be He þa gefeng..., which is invariably the form with a personal pronoun; the 'he' in this verse is better omitted.

13. In the *cóm þa* form the adverb is enclitic to the verb and normally unstressed, the only exception being when the last syllable of the verb is itself unstressed and *þa* is immediately followed by the caesural pause, in which case the adverb retains its stress, e.g.

620   ymbeode þá   ides Helminga;

there are at least nine certain instances of this form in *Beowulf.*

In the *he þá* form the subject-pronoun is proclitic to the adverb (128) and unstressed. If there is a governed pronoun besides the subject-pronoun, it stands after the stressed *þa*; at least this is the normal order in Ælfric, where sentences like 'hi þa him and-wyrdon' abound, and it should probably be restored in

2490   ic him ða maðmas. . .geald æt guðe.

The inversion occurs also in

28   hi hine.ða ætbæron   to brimes faroðe,

where, however, *hi* has no noun of reference (41) and *hine ða* may be right without *hi* (cf. 2720 below), 'gesiðas' being the subject; the verse, as it stands, gives us an abnormal trisyllabic anacrusis in an A type (see 161).

If the subject is a noun, a governed pronoun may stand first, e.g.

340   Him ða ellenrof   andswarode,
                wlanc Wedera leod,
2720   Hyne ða mid handa. . .wætere gelafede | ðegn

14. When the adverb *ða* is not the headword, it is frequently found in the poem qualifying a stressed verb, especially in sentences beginning with *ond*, e.g.

630   ond þa gyddode   guðe gefysed.

In such sentences *ða* seems to be used, like the Latin *tum demum*, with special significance to mark the crowning act of a series, as in

1043   Ond ða Beowulfe   bega gehwæþres
                eodor Ingwina   onweald geteah,
                wicga ond wæpna;

where the preceding twenty-two lines have described the bringing
in of the gifts; or

2933   ond ða folgode   feorhgeniðlan,
              oð ðæt hi oðeodon   earfoðlice
              in Hrefnesholt   hlafordlease.

which follows the description of Ongentheow's defeat of the Geats
near Ravenswood. Similarly 'ond þa' would be very appropriate
in the short line

2195   ond him gesealde   seofon ðusendo,

and also in

3169   þa ymbe hlæw riodan   hildediore

where the 'ride round the tomb' is the climax of the burial
ceremonies; a subordinate *ða*-clause is meaningless in the
context.

15. *Ða wæs*. In prose this sentence-form, like *ða com*, is ambivalent, though predominantly a principal sentence. In *Beowulf*
the subordinate clause is almost as common as the principal
sentence, especially in *b* verses, e.g. 917, ða wæs morgen leoht,
1008 þa wæs sæl ond mæl, where we have the normal transition-
clause (104); here again metre supports sense, since *þa* must be the
unstressed conjunction unless it can be shown that a 3-lift *b* verse
was admissible. Why do editors point 467 ða wæs Heregar dead
as a principal sentence but 2372 ða wæs Hygelac dead as a
subordinate clause? Sense and metre alike indicate subordination
in both.

In principal sentences of the *þa wæs* form the stressed adverb,
in verse as in prose, is always the headword; *wæs þa* (see 62) is not
simply a variant of *ða wæs*, but something quite different. It is
noteworthy that in *Beowulf* the subject of the verb is always a
noun and never, as it may be in prose, a pronoun (e.g. þa wæs he
on salum). The regular negative form is *næs þá*, as in

3126   Næs ða on hlytme   hwa þæt hord strude

'Then was there no need to cast lots who should rifle that
hoard.'

The reader should observe that the ambivalence of *ða wæs* is true only of the sentence in its written form; in speech the stressed adverb must always have been distinguished from the unstressed conjunction.

16. *The Correlation Rule.* In verse, as in prose other than Charters and similar bald records, it may be taken as a general rule that, wherever we have two *þa*-sentences in sequence, there is a *þa...þa* correlation and that one of the sentences, usually the first, is subordinate to the other and should be so punctuated. The reader will find examples from prose in *SS* 11, and here are some from *Beowulf*:

126   Ða wæs on uhtan   mid ærdæge
        Grendles guðcræft   gumum undyrne;
        Ða wæs æfter wiste   wop up ahafen,

'When at dawn Grendel's war-power became manifest, then after feasting was lamentation raised'; for the ictus on the conjunction in 126 (only at the beginning of a line), see 134.

1644   Ða com in gan   ealdor ðegna...,
        hæle hildedeor   Hroðgar gretan.
        Ða wæs be feaxe   on flet boren
        Grendles heafod,

'When the chieftain had entered to greet Hrothgar, then was G.'s head brought into hall.'

2752   Ða ic snude gefrægn   sunu Wihstanes
                           ...hringnet beran,
        brogdne beadusercean,   under beorges hrof.
        Geseah ða sigehreðig...

'So soon as W.'s son had come in his mailed coat beneath the barrow's roof, then saw he, victorious, many a treasure.'

3134   Ða wæs wunden gold   on wæn hladen...
        Him ða gegiredan   Geata leode | ad

'When the twisted gold was loaded on the wain, then did the people of the Geats make ready for him a funeral pyre.'

These four pairs of correlated sentences are transformed by the usual punctuation into four pairs of 'then' sentences; it may be observed, incidentally, that 1644 and 2752 confirm the subordinate character of the *ða com* and *ða ic gefrægn* types. In

1274   Ða he hean gewat,
mancynnes feond,   ond his modor ða gyt
    ...gegan wolde

ond spoils the correlation and should be ejected. For *siððan-ða* correlation see 28.

Let us consider an example where correlation is not the right way of dealing with a sequence of *ða*-sentences:

1397   Ahleop ða se gomela,   Gode þancode
                   ...þæs se man gespræc.
     Ða wæs Hroðgare   hors gebæted,
     wicg wundenfeax.   Wisa fengel
     geatolic gende.

Here the first is a principal sentence of the *com ða* form which regularly follows the end of a speech; the second is not another principal sentence, but the usual major transition-clause (103), marking a new action and a change of scene to the mere: 'The old King leapt up and thanked God for what the hero had spoken. When Hrothgar's horse had been bridled, the wise prince rode forth in state [and] his foot-troop of shieldmen strode beside him.' The same problem arises in

26   Him ða Scyld gewat   to gescæphwile...
     [hi] hine ða ætbæron   to brimes faroðe
     swæse gesiðas,

but here an *opening* transition-clause is wanted, cf. 662 ða him Hroðgar gewat; by reading 'ða him Scyld gewat' we get a good correlation. The *reflexive* 'him' in a *him ða* principal sentence is a solecism.

17. We may conclude this survey with contrasted versions of a few other *ða*-sentences of various kinds; the P. versions are from R. K. Gordon's literal translation of the *Beowulf* text, as usually punctuated, in Dent's *Everyman* series; and the S. versions are the same but with the subordinations suggested in this chapter.

A comparison may help the reader to decide which better represent a work of literary art:

Line 461, cited in **3**:

P. Then the race of the Weders would not receive him. Thence he sought the people of the South-Danes. Then I had just begun to rule the Danish people.

S. Since the race of the Weders, etc., he departed thence to the South-Dane people just when I began to rule them.

Line 579, cited in **3**:

P. Yet I escaped with my life from the grasp of foes, weary of travel. Then the sea...bore me to shore in the land of the Finns.

S. Yet I escaped..., weary of travel when the sea cast me up among the Finns.

Line 662, cited in **6**:

P. Then H. went his way out of the hall; the warlike king was minded to seek W. the queen for his bedfellow. The glorious king had set a hall-guardian against Grendel.

S. See **6**.

Line 1274, cited in **3**:

P. Then he departed, the foe of mankind, in misery...and his mother then still purposed to go [to avenge her son].

S. When *he* departed in misery, his mother still purposed to go to avenge her son.

(The right form for a principal sentence is 'he ða hean gewat' as in 1263; the clause, as it stands, is subordinate, and *ond* is meaningless; see **16**.)

Lines 1596–1601, cited in **8** and **11**:

P. (Said) they did not expect to see the chieftain again. Then it seemed to many that the sea-wolf had slain him. Then came the ninth hour of the day. The bold Scyldings forsook the headland.

S. They did not expect to see the chieftain again since it seemed to many that the sea-wolf had slain him. When came the ninth hour, the bold S. left the headland.

Perhaps the most astonishing thing about these *ða*-sentences is the double assumption usually implied by the accepted punctuation, viz. (1) that the only word-order which is unambiguously subordinate in OE prose could be freely used by a poet in principal sentences (e.g. Ða hine Wedera cyn habban ne mihte, Ða mec sæ oðbær, Ða him Hroðgar gewat, Ða ðæs monige gewearð); (2) that nevertheless the adverb *ða* in such sentences could be stressed or unstressed at pleasure (see **126**).

Ðonne-sentences

18. Instances of demonstrative order in a principal sentence, where the verb is stressed, are only apparent; some of them can be explained, like the similar *ða*-sentences, as subordinate clauses, e.g.

377   Ðonne sægdon ðæt   sæliðende...
                                Hine halig God
        for arstafum   us onsende

'Since sea-farers have said [that he has the strength of ten] God of his grace must have sent him to us'; 'then' is meaningless in the context. In some, e.g.

525   Ðonne wene ic to ðe   wyrsan geðingea

the *ðonne* (adv.) is not temporal. In

2041   Ðonne cwið æt beore   seðe beah gesyhð,
                    ...ond ðæt word acwyð,

the tautological repetition of the verb cannot be right, whatever the remedy. We have, however, in

3107   ond ðonne geferian   frean userne,

where *ðonne* is not the headword, a veritable instance of demonstrative order with the climactic sense commented on in **14**: 'and then let us bear our lord to his funeral'. There is nothing irregular in the order after the adverb in

1106   ðonne hit sweordes ecg   syððan scolde,
2446   ðonne he gyd wrece,
        sarigne sang,   ðonne his sunu hangað,

since in both, *ðæt* and not *ðonne* is the headword (see **58**).

Demonstrative order with an unstressed verb is common, e.g.

484   Ðonne wæs ðeos medoheal,   ðonne dæg lixte,
               ...blode bestymed.

'Ever was this meadhall, when daylight appeared, besprent with blood.'

19. With a past tense *ðonne* always has a frequentative meaning in OE; there are some passages in *Beowulf* in which this sense is important, e.g.

1066 ðonne (on) healgamen Hroðgares scop
    æfter medobence mænan scolde...

Here the use of *ðonne* rather than *ða* is good evidence that the Finn-story was told by the bard in more than one 'lay':

1143 ðonne him Hunlafing hildeleoman
    on bearm dyde;

'Whenever Hunlafing gave him possession of a sword.' Perhaps the act would not be repeated by any one individual; if so, 'a Hunlafing' may be meant, i.e. one of a family of that name.

1486 ðæt ic gumcystum godne funde
    beaga bryttan, breac ðonne (ic) moste

Here 'whenever' does not appear to have a meaning; the conjunction elsewhere, e.g. in 1177 bruc ðenden ðu mote, is always *ðenden*, and *ðonne* may be an echo of the two *ðonnes* just above. In

2633 Ic ðæt mæl geman, þær we medu þegun,
    þonne we geheton ussum hlaforde...
    þæt we him ða guðgeatwa gyldan woldon,

the frequentative 'þonne' contradicts the singular noun 'þæt mæl', which should obviously be a plural; in the lines

Mald. 212 Gemunu ða mæla þe we oft æt meodo spræcon,
    þonne we on bence beot ahofon

we have, no doubt, an imitation of the *Beowulf* passage; and the first line, however it be corrected, at least confirms the suggestion of a plural noun in *Beowulf* 2633. And in

3051 þonne wæs þæt yrfe eacencræftig,
    iumonna gold galdre bewunden,

the interpretation by some editors 'then (i.e. when the hoard was laid in earth)' cannot be right unless there was more than one inhumation; it seems best to make the sentence a dependent clause and the conjunction causal 'since the great inheritance had been placed under a spell'.

20. Of the correlation rule we have a clear example in

1741   þonne se weard swefeð,
        sawele hyrde;   bið se slæp to fæst,
        bisgum gebunden,   bona swiðe neah,
        se þe of flanbogan   fyrenum sceoteð.
        Ðonne bið on hreþre   under helm drepen...

for, if we substitute commas for the major stops, and make the first 'þonne' a conjunction with three co-ordinate clauses ('se weard swefeð', 'bið se slæp to fæst', '[bið] bona neah') and the second 'þonne' the correlative adverb, we have good syntax and good sense: 'when the watcher, the guardian of the soul, slumbers, when the sleep is too heavy and the slayer very near that shoots wickedly from his bow, then is he (the prosperous man) stricken to the heart....'

Ðær-sentences

21. Many sentences with conjunctive order, which are really subordinate, are taken by editors as principal sentences. In some of them *ðær* has an obvious antecedent as a relative, e.g.

493   [benc] ðær swiðferhðe   sittan eodon,

512   þa git on sund reon;
        þær git eagorstream   earmum þehton,

976   in nidgripe   nearwe befongen,
        balwon bendum;   ðær abidan sceal
        maga mane fah   miclan domes,

1242   Setton him to heafdon   hilderandas,
        bordwudu beorhtan;   ðær on bence wæs...
        heaþosteapa helm

1364   wudu wyrtum fæst   wæter oferhelmað.
        Ðær (man) mæg nihta gehwæm   niðwundor seon,

2135   Ic ða ðæs wælmes...grundhyrde fond.
        Ðær unc hwile wæs   hand gemæne;

2367   Oferswam ða sioleða bigong...eft to leodum;
        þær him Hygd gebead   hord ond rice

2213   stanbeorh steapne;   stig under læg
             eldum uncuð.   Ðær on innan giong
             niðða nathwylc,

2241   Beorh eallgearo...;
             Ðær on innan bær   eorlgestreona
             hringa hyrde

In the last two *ðær on innan* (=whereinto) is the relative, not the demonstrative, adverb, as the unstressed *ðær* shows, 'beorh' being the antecedent in both places (see further 81).

22. Sometimes *ðær* has its idiomatic quasi-temporal or other extended sense (when, if), as in

439   ic sceal ymb feorh sacan
            lað wið laðum;   ðær gelyfan sceal
            Dryhtnes dome   se þe hine deað nimeð.

549   Wæs merefixa   mod onhrered;
            þær me wið laðum   licsyrce min
                 ...helpe gefremede,

773   ac he ðæs fæste wæs...
            searoþoncum besmiþod.   Ðær fram sylle abeag
            medubenc monig

793   ne his lifdagas   leoda ænigum
            nytte tealde.   Ðær genehost brægd
            eorl Beowulfes   ealde lafe,

852   feorh alegde,
            hæðene sawle;   ðær him hel onfeng.

2570   Scyld wel gebearg
            life ond lice   læssan hwile...;
            ðær he þy fyrste   forman dogore
            wealdan moste,   swa him wyrd ne gescraf
            hreð æt hilde.

23. The superstition, which disallows subordination in a clause preceding the principal sentence (see 2) evidently extends to *ðær*, for the clauses which the accepted text admits all follow the principal sentence. Let us take some examples in which the clause comes first, if rightly understood:

1190   þær se goda sæt,
            Beowulf Geata,   be þæm gebroðrum twæm.
            Him wæs ful boren,

'Where, by the two brothers, the hero Beowulf sat, the cup was

brought to him'; this is the sense we expect, whereas there is none
if we take 'þær se goda sæt' as a principal sentence.

1269   þær him aglæca   ætgræpe wearð;
         hwæþre he gemunde   mægenes strenge,

'Even when the monster was at grips with him, he yet remembered
the might of his strength'; for this use of *hwæþre* (=nevertheless)
after a subordinate clause, cf. 1716 Ðeah hine mihtig God forð
gefremede, hwæðere him greow breosthord blodreow.

1470   þær he dome forleas,
         ellenmærðum.   Ne wæs þæm oðrum swa,
         syðþan he hine to guðe   gegyred hæfde.

'Whereas hé (Unferth) lost honour, the glory of prowess, 'twas
far otherwise with Beowulf when he had girded himself for battle.'
In the last two examples *þær* has a sense in the context which
shades off into the concessive.

We have, lastly, an example of correlation, where as usual the
subordinate clause comes first:

2075   ðær we gesunde   sæl weardodon.
         Ðær wæs Hondscio   hild onsæge...

'Where wé kept watch in the hall unharmed, there did battle
prove fatal to H.'

24. *Ðær wæs*, like *ða wæs*, is ambivalent. In *a* verses it is
usually a principal sentence, the stress on the adverb being
certified by the metre in lines like

847   Ðær wæs on blode   brim weallende.

Metre tolerates the stressed adverb in *b* verses like 835 ðær wæs
eal geador (Dx), but most of the *b* verses are of the metrical type
seen in

35   on bearm scipes,
         mærne be mæste.   Ðær wæs maðma fela...
88   dream gehyrde
         hludne in healle;   ðær wæs hearpan sweg...
496   Scop hwilum sang
         hador on Heorote.   Ðær wæs hæleða dream...,
1232   Eode þa to setle.   Ðær wæs symbla cyst...

where *ðær* must be a relative, and the sentence subordinate, unless it can be shown that a 3-lift *b* verse was admissible; sense supports the relative *ðær*, for in all these verses there is an obvious antecedent to it. For the problem of expletive *ðær* see **73**.

25. Of demonstrative order with a *stressed* verb, e.g. ðær geseah he, there is no instance in *Beowulf*; and of the alternative forms corresponding to *com ða, he ða*, the first fails altogether (though we have an instance in *Mald.* 64 Ne mihte ðær for wætere werod to þam oðrum) and the second is comparatively rare: examples are

913	He ðær eallum wearð... freondum gefægra (see, however, **185**);
2009	Ic ðær furðum cwom...

CHAPTER III

SENTENCES INTRODUCED BY
ÆR, NU, SIÐÐAN, ETC.

26. In prose, homographs (other than *þa, þonne, þær*) which can
be either adverbs or conjunctions are usually followed, as adverbs,
by common order and, as conjunctions, by conjunctive order
(*SS* 35); the usage in verse is the same except that certain of the
adverbs, e.g. *nu, swa, forðam*, which even in prose, when headwords, are occasionally followed by conjunctive order, exhibit
this order normally in verse, as in

1769	Swa ic Hring-Dena	hund missera
	weold under wolcnum	

There are, however, places in which such words are better taken
as conjunctions, even when the order allows an adverbial sense,
as in

1342	se þe æfter sincgyfan	on sefan greoteð—
	...;	*nu* seo hand ligeð,

'now that the hand is numb...'; and so in the long sentence

2047	Meaht ðu, min wine,	mece gecnawan...?
	Nu her þara banena	byre nathwylces
	frætwum hremig	on flet gæð,

'now that the son of one of those murderers steps here into hall,
glorying in the weapon', and in

470	*Siððan* ða fæhðe	feo ðingode;
	sende ic Wylfingum...ealde maðmas	

'After [he] had settled the feud with money', or 'after money
had settled the feud'.

2739		Ic þæs ealles mæg
	feorhbennum seoc	gefean habban;
	forðan me witan ne ðearf	Waldend fira | morðorbealo

'because the Ruler of men may not blame me for murder'; subordination seems to be demanded by the sense in all these.

27. As in prose, subordination is particularly appropriate when a *nu*-sentence is followed either (i) by a verb in the imperative mood, e.g.

1376   Nu is se ræd gelang
        eft æt þe anum...;   sec gif þu dyrre

'Since help must come once more from thee alone, seek if thou dare' (on this sentence see further **178**).

2646   Nu is se dæg cumen,
        þæt ure mandryhten   mægenes behofað,
        godra guðrinca;   wutun gongan to,

'Now that the day is come when our lord needs the strength of good warriors, let us go to his help...'; or (ii) by a correlated *nu*, e.g.

251   Nu ic eower sceal
        frumcyn witan...Nú ge feorbuend,
                ...minne gehyrað
        anfealdne geþoht;

'Since I must know of your lineage ére ye fare further, hear now, O far-dwellers, my plain thought.'

424   ond nu wið Grendel sceal,
        wið þam aglæcan   ana gehegan
        ðing wið þyrse.   Ic þe nú ða
                ...biddan wille,

'And since I must hold debate alone with Grendel, I would now beg thee....'

Is it, once more, because these clauses precede the principal sentences, that they are disallowed in all four editions?

28. The Correlation Rule can guide us to a right construction when applied to other correlatives besides *nu*; some examples are

2071   to hwan sýððan wearð
        hondræs hæleða.   Syððan heofones gim
        glad ofer grundas

'What was the outcome of the struggle after the jewel of heaven glided away.'

2200   Eft þæt geiode   ufaran dogrum
               hildehlæmmum,   syððan Hygelac læg...—:
               sýððan Beowulfe   brade rice
               on hand gehwearf.

'It came to pass in later days *that*, after H. fell, the broad realm then passed into Beowulf's hands' (see further 33).

3066   Swá wæs Biowulfe...
               swa hit oð domes dæg   diope benemdon
               þeodnas mære,

'It befell B. just as the great princes had solemnly pronounced the curse....'

1927   ðeah ðe wintra lyt
             under burhlocan   gebiden hæbbe,
             Hæreðes dohtor;   næs hio hnah swa ðéah,

'Though H.'s daughter had dwelt few winters within castle walls, yet was she no niggard.' All these passages need repunctuation.

Siððan is occasionally correlated with the adverb *ða*, as in

1261   siððan Cain wearð
            to ecgbanan   angan breðer
               ...;   he ða fag gewat
           morðre gemearcod

'After Cain had slain his own brother, he then departed branded with murder.'

1556   siððan he eft astod,
           geseah ða on searwum   sigeeadig bil

'When he stood up again, he saw a victorious sword'; in both places the *siððan*-clause is usually attached by editors to the sentence before.

29. The conjunction *swa* has several shades of meaning and, in particular, an idiomatic causal sense, as in

880   ðonne he swulces hwæt   secgan wolde,
           eam his nefan,   swa hie a wæron
           æt niða gehwam   nydgesteallan;

'Seeing that they were always comrades at need in every contest.'
So also in

2442   sceolde hwæðre swaðeah. . . ealdres linnan.
        Swa bið geomorlic gomelum ceorle. . .

'yet must he needs pass from life unavenged, seeing that it is sad
for an aged man to endure that his son should hang'; and so
probably in

2142   ac me eorla hleo   eft gesealde
        maðma menigeo,   maga Healfdenes.
        Swa se ðeodkyning   þeawum lyfde;

'but Healfdene's son bestowed on me many a treasure, like the
generous king he ever was.' There seems to be no good reason,
however, for assuming a vaguer sense (e.g. 'indeed') of *forðam* in
some contexts; it will always bear the meaning 'therefore' or
'because' according as it is adverb or conjunction.

30. Correlative words like *ær, nu, siððan, swa,* in Old as in
Modern English, are stressed as adverbs and unstressed as conjunctions (see further **124**). We have obvious examples of the
stressed adverb *siððan* in

142   heold hyne syððan,
1901   swurd gesealde,   ðæt he syððan wæs | weorðra;

in many such lines, as in 1901, the adverb alliterates. The difference
of stress often provides a decisive test of the construction in
places where it is in dispute; in each of the lines

6   syððan ærest wearð | funden
850   siððan dreama leas
        in fenfreoðo   feorh alegde,
1235   syððan æfen cwom,
1689   syððan flod ofsloh
        giganta cyn,

at least two editors take *siððan* as the adverb, but metre disallows
this if the rule forbidding a 3-lift *b* verse is valid.

On the other hand, in the three *swa*-clauses in **29** the metrical
test does not help us, since the verses scan equally well with a

stressed *swa* (as Dx) or with an unstressed *swa* (as C, B, C). In such places idiom alone is the deciding factor.

31. This is a convenient place to say a few words about the consecutive *þæt*-clauses in *Beowulf* which must strike every reader as a characteristic feature of style. In OE prose the clause is common after the adverb *swa*, either alone (*swa ðæt*) or in combination with an adjective as in 'swa bilewite þæt hie ne cuðon nan þing yfeles', but it is exceedingly rare without *swa*; in poetry, and especially in *Beowulf*, the converse is the case, as there are only one or two examples of the clause after *swa* (1732 swa gewealdene þæt...), but examples abound of the construction without, e.g.

2527   Ic eom on mode from,
        þæt ic wið þone guðflogan   gylp ofersitte.

'I am stout of heart, so that I forgo boasting against the war-flier.' ModE idiom might express the relation of the second clause to the first by a co-ordinate clause 'I am stout of heart *and* forgo...', and this is the normal construction in mature OE prose also; examples may be found on almost any page of Ælfric, e.g. *Hom.* I. 454 ft. þa adumbode se deofol *and* ne mihte nanum þara gehelpan, 458. 14 heo bat ond totær ælcne þe heo geræcan mihte *and* hire nan man genealæcan ne dorste, where poetic idiom would write 'ðæt he ne mihte...gehelpan' and 'ðæt hire nan...genealæcan ne dorste'.

There are in *Beowulf* two kinds of context in which such a *ðæt*-clause is particularly idiomatic: (i) after a verb of motion, e.g.

358   eode ellenrof,   ðæt he for eaxlum gestod

'He went *and* stood, gallant man, before his shoulder' and so in 221, 404, 1316, 2716, and possibly 1913 Ceol up geðrang, on lande stod, where Sievers inserts 'ðæt he' before 'on'; (ii) after verbs of assailing, e.g.

1540   brægd ða beadwe heard...ðæt heo on flet gebeah.

'Stern in battle, he swung her, *and* she fell to the ground', and so in 1544, 2918, 2974; the verb in the *ðæt*-clause is usually 'bugan', and in

2977 Let se hearda Higelaces þegn
    eald sweord eotonisc entiscne helm
    brecan ofer bordweal; ða gebeah cyning,

the idiom cries aloud for *þæt* instead of *þa*, which, as a continuative conjunction (4), is very dubious and, as a stressed adverb, is forbidden by the metre.

32. There are many places in *Beowulf* where we have two *þæt*-clauses in sequence, e.g.

771 Ða wæs wundor micel, þæt se winsele
    wiðhæfde heaþodeorum, þæt he on hrusan ne feol....

How are these to be construed? Is the second *þæt* an anaphoric repetition of the first in the sense of 'and' as in 'Ye know that she is fair, That she is kind'? Or is the second *þæt*-clause not coordinate but subordinate to the first and to be construed in a consecutive sense 'it was great wonder that the wine-hall withstood their rage so that it fell not to earth'? There is hardly a trace in OE prose or verse of the kind of anaphora mentioned (see further 112), and since the second construction suits every context there can be little doubt that it is the right one. Other exx. are

890 hwæþre him gesælde, ðæt þæt swurd þurhwod
    wrætlicne wyrm, þæt hit on wealle ætstod,

'that his sword went through the worm so that it was fixed in the wall.'

1085   ac hig him geþingo budon,
   þæt hie him oðer flet eal gerymdon,
     ...þæt hie healfre geweald | agan moston

'that they should clear a hall for them so that they might have power over half the....' Sometimes both clauses are of the same kind, e.g.

2747 Bio nu on ofoste, þæt ic ærwelan,
    goldæht ongite..., ðæt ic ðy seft mæge
    lif alætan

where a second final clause is dependent on the first: 'haste now that I may see the ancient wealth, so that I may leave life more easily.' In one passage

2698
      þær he his mæges healp,
þæt he þone niðgæst   nioðor hwene sloh,
secg on searwum,   þæt ðæt sweord gedeaf
fah ond fæted,   þæt ðæt fyr ongon
sweðrian syððan,

we have three *þæt*-clauses in sequence, all consecutive, making a very cumbrous chain of subordination. Here Sievers' emendation 'Ða ðæt fyr ongon', correlative to 'þa gen self cyning geweold his gewitte' which follows, gives us both better syntactical articulation and better sense; and probably a sequence of two *ðæt*-clauses was the limit everywhere in *Beowulf*.

33. The position of the conjunction *ðæt* introducing a noun-clause in Old English is important. The rule is that it always stands immediately before its own clause, so that, if this is modified by other, e.g. adverbial, clauses, these are placed before and not, as in Modern English, after the conjunction. This can be clearly seen from the many instances in the mature prose of Ælfric, e.g. *Hom*. I. 82. 12 ðohte gif he ealle ofsloge *ðæt* se an ne ætburste ðe he sohte 'thinking *that*, if he slew them all, the one that he sought for could not escape'. An inspection of the poet's usage in *Beowulf* will show the reader how carefully he observed the rule, e.g.

1474
Geþenc nu, se mæra...hwæt wit geo spræcon,
gif ic æt þearfe   ðinre scolde
aldre linnan,   ðæt þu me a wære
forð gewitenum   on fæder stæle.

'Consider now, O prince; what we spake just now, *that*, if I must depart from life in thy cause, thou wouldst be to me as a father when I am gone'; here, as in prose, the conjunction is properly placed before the noun-clause and not before 'gif'.

34. In two, or possibly three, places, in *Beowulf* the conjunction is missing, the most striking instance being in the lines already cited in 28:

2200
    Eft ðæt geiode   ufaran dogrum
    hildehlæmmum,   syððan Hygelac læg,...
    ða hyne gesohtan   on sigeðeode
    hearde hildefrecan,   Heaðo-Scilfingas,
    niða genægdan   nefan Hererices—:
    syððan Beowulfe   brade rice
    on hand gehwearf;

where the poet's usage demands a *ðæt* before the second 'syððan'. The question therefore arises whether the conjunction could be omitted.

Three editors defend its absence by the analogy of a similar omission after *cwæð*. Let us therefore consider the construction of this verb in *Beowulf*. The conjunction is omitted when, and only when, the subject of the subordinate clause is the same as that of *cwæð*, e.g. in sentences like

199   cwæð, he guðcyning   secean wolde,

but not in sentences like

92   cwæð ðæt se Ælmihtiga   eorðan worhte.

The clauses without *ðæt* are, in fact, a real exception and well illustrate the adage *Exceptio probat regulam*. They are not found even after other verbs of saying, e.g. *secgan*; how can they justify the sporadic omission of *ðæt* after quite different verbs and before clauses in which the subject is *not* the same? The general rule is valid for these, and *ðæt* should be restored wherever it is missing; it may be observed that in the eighteen instances of the construction in *Andreas* the conjunction never fails. No doubt the late position of the conjunction in some of the instances in *Beowulf* explains its being dropped by the scribe.

CHAPTER IV

DEMONSTRATIVE AND RELATIVE PRONOUNS

35. 'In prose no part of the demonstrative pronoun *se, seo, ðæt* other than the neuter nominative can stand at the head of a sentence except as the antecedent, and any supposed instance to the contrary is really a relative pronoun (*SS* 48).' We have to enquire whether the rule is valid in *Beowulf* also, i.e. whether supposed exceptions admit of the alternative construction mentioned:

(i) *Se* (*seo*) is usually taken as the demonstrative in

196	[Higelaces þegn]; se wæs moncynnes	mægenes strengest.
469	[bearn Healfdenes]; se wæs betera ðonne ic.	
898	[Wælses eafera;] wyrm hat gemealt.	
	Se wæs wreccena wide mærost	
2024	[dohtor Hroðgares]. Sio gehaten is	
	...gladum suna Frodan.	
2087	[Glof]; sio wæs orðoncum eall gegyrwed	
2391	[god cyning]. Se ðæs leodhryres lean gemunde	
2412	[hlæw];...Se wæs innan full	
	wrætta ond wira	
2804	[hlæw]; se scel to gemyndum minum leodum	
	heah hlifian	
3042	[legdraca]; se wæs fiftiges fotgemearces	
	lang on legere;	

These all admit of the alternative construction as relative clauses; they are, however, punctuated in the editions as principal sentences, and the editors may fairly be asked why the supposed demonstrative *se* never occurs except where there is an obvious antecedent. The only passage which is not quite straightforward is 898; here, if the antecedent is 'eafera', the sentence 'wyrm hat gemealt' must, as the text stands, be taken as a parenthesis. The construction is ambiguous in

1296	Se wæs Hroðgare	hæleþa leofost...
	rice randwiga,	ðone ðe heo on ræste abreat,

where 'se' may be taken as antecedent to the pleonastic relative 'ðone ðe'; but it is also possible to construe it as a relative with 'anne' in the sentence before as its antecedent, in which case the antecedent to 'ðone ðe' is 'randwiga'. In 2024 'sio gehaten is' is the second of two relative clauses after 'dohtor', the first being 'ða ic Freaware nemnan hyrde'. The double relative after the same antecedent is so common even in prose that it should need no illustration, but two examples may be given:

ASC 890. Godrum ðæs fulluht-nama wæs Æþelstan se wæs Ælfredes godsunu.

Oros. 129. 24. ane ea sio hæfde ungemettlice ceald wæter seo wæs Ciðnus haten.

It should be noted that the conjunctive order itself disallows 'sio gehaten is' as a principal sentence. For 3042 see also **121**.

36. The examples from *Beowulf* in the last section are not different in word-order or other essential respects from the eleven sentences from *Orosius* cited in *SS* 43 *a*, all of which translate a Latin relative clause. This test fails us in *Beowulf*, but the metrical test may serve us equally well, for wherever *se* is indubitably demonstrative, e.g. as the antecedent, the stress is always certified by the metre, as in

44	ðonne ðá dydon	
	ðe hine forð onsendon...	
2406	Sé wæs on ðam ðreate	ðreotteoða secg
	se ðæs orleges	or onstealde,
3009	ond ðóne gebringan	ðe us beagas geaf.

In *b* verses, however, like 469 se wæs betera ðonne ic, 2024 sio gehaten is, 2412 se wæs innan full, where editors make *se* demonstrative, it will not bear this stress unless it can be shown that a 3-lift *b* verse was admissible. There are, moreover, many striking inconsistencies in the editors' treatment of the clauses we are considering; on what principle, for example, do they make

2391   Se ðæs leodhryres   lean gemunde

a principal sentence, and the exactly similar sentence-form just

below, 2407 se ðæs orleges or onstealde, a subordinate clause?
The same question may be asked about the pair

2024   sio gehaten is...gladum suna Frodan,
789   se ðe manna wæs   mægene strengest,

and many others.

37. (ii) An oblique case of *se, seo, ðæt,* where it is the headword,
is taken by editors as the demonstrative pronoun in

12	[cyning]. Ðæm eafera wæs æfter cenned
59	[Healfdene]. Ðæm feower bearn...in worold wocun
194	[Gewin]. Ðæt fram ham gefrægn Higelaces þegn
587	þeah ðu þinum broðrum to banan wurde, heafodmægum; þæs þu in helle scealt werhðo dreogan
1037	[eahta mearas]; þara anum stod sadol searwum fah
1145	[billa selest]; þæs wæron mid Eotenum ecge cuðe.
1273	[are] ...; ðy he þone feond ofercwom
1349	[ellorgæstas]. Ðæra oðer wæs... | idese onlicnes.
1354	[oðer]; þone on geardagum Grendel nemdon foldbuende
1363	[Se mere]; ofer þæm hongiað hrinde bearwas
2148	[maðmas]; ða ic ðe, beorncyning, bringan wylle
2194	[Hreðles lafe]; þæt he on Biowulfes bearm alegde
2479	Ðæt mægwine mine gewræcan
2612	[Eanmundes]; þam æt sæcce wearð ...Weohstan bana
2616	[eald sweord]; þæt him Onela forgeaf
2629	; ðæt se wyrm onfand
2769	[segn]; of ðam leoma stod
3014	[beagas]; þa sceal brond fretan

These, like the last group, admit of the alternative construction.
In all but three of them the pronoun as a relative has an obvious
noun-antecedent. The antecedent in 2194 should by the sense be
'lafe', and *ðæt,* unless a misreading of *ðe,* must have been attracted
into the gender of 'sweordes' in the parenthetic line just before
(see **71**); for 194 see further **101**. The neuter relative in 588,
2479 and 2629 is idiomatic *without* antecedent, in Old as in Modern

English, when referring to the action predicated in the preceding sentence: 'for which (i.e. the slaying of thy brother) thou shalt suffer damnation in hell', 'all which (i.e. the malicious slaying) my kinsmen-friends avenged', 'which (=as) the worm discovered' (in 2479 ðæt might perhaps be taken as the consecutive conjunction). All the exx. in this section thus conform strictly to the prose rule, if the pronouns are taken as relatives.

It should be noted that there is nothing abnormal in the order in

942   Hwæt, ðæt secgan mæg
    efne swa hwylc mægða...

2864 Ðæt, la, mæg secgan se ðe wyle soð specan,

where the front-position of the demonstrative is influenced, as in OE prose, by the interjection, cf. *Hom.* I. 78. 28 Hwæt, ða God on swefne hi gewarnode; without interjection the order (see 40) would be 'Mæg ðæt', as in

2032 Mæg ðæs ofþyncan ðeoden Heaðo-Beardna.

38. (iii) The neuter nominative ðæt in the sentence-form ðæt *is* may, like *se*, be either the demonstrative antecedent or the relative; in

1455 Næs þæt þonne mætost mægenfultuma,
   þæt him on ðearfe lah ðyle Hroðgares;

it is the antecedent (ðæt ðæt=that which); in the following it is the neuter relative:

454 hrægla selest; þæt is Hrædlan laf.

Most frequently, however, in this sentence-form, ðæt is a demonstrative of *general* reference as in ModE, e.g.

170 Ðæt wæs wræc micel wine Scyldinga
2999 Ðæt ys sio fæhðo...

where it refers, not to any particular noun, but to an action or event described or implied in the preceding sentence: 'all this was a great affliction to the prince'.

Ðæt cannot therefore be used, in a mere statement of identity, to refer to a person, as it is in

348 Wulfgar maþelode,—þæt wæs Wendla leod;

here, if the pronoun is intended as a demonstrative, it should be
'he' (41); if as a relative, an idiomatic form of it after a proper
noun both in prose and verse is ðe, as in

499   Unferð maþelode,   Ecglafes bearn,
           þe æt fotum sæt   frean Scyldinga:

and 'þæt' in 348 probably stands for 'ðe' (see 172).

39. How then, it will be asked, is a passage like the following to
be interpreted?

249   nis þæt seldguma,
           wæpnum geweorðad,   næfne him his wlite leoge;

here ðæt must not be construed as though it were *he*; it carries us
back to the sentence before, from which it takes its meaning:
'that (=such as I describe) is no retainer decked out with arms,
unless his looks belie him'. And so in

11   þæt wæs god cyning

where ðæt means 'such a character, i.e. one that throve in honour',
and in

1610   onwindeð wælrapas,   se geweald hafað
           sæla ond mæla;   þæt is soð Metod.

where ðæt is again defined by the sentence before 'when he that
holds power over times and seasons unwinds the water-fetters;
that is true God!' The modern 'Help me, that's a good fellow' no
doubt traces its descent from the OE usage. The ðæt may be
defined by a following clause, e.g.

1372   Nis ðæt heoru stow.
           Ðonon yðgeblond   up astigeð,

where 'ðonon' is a relative.

On the other hand in

1074   hie on gebyrd hruron
           gare wunde;   þæt wæs geomuru ides!
1812   nales wordum log
           meces ecge;   þæt wæs modig secg.

the general reference fails and the context is quite different; it
suggests rather the idiomatic consecutive clause (31), which gives

the expected sense: 'and (=so that) a sad lady was she', 'and a proud man was he', the *grammatical* subjects being 'ides' and 'secg'. In some sentences, e.g.

1255	ðæt gesyne wearð
2327	Ðæt ðam godan wæs
	hreow on hreðre

the word-order itself forbids a principal sentence; the first is again a consecutive clause, and possibly the second also.

40. So far we have been concerned with the pronoun *se, seo, ðæt* as headword in a sentence. Internally, in *Beowulf* as in prose (*SS* 51), the demonstrative is freely used in the oblique cases of all numbers and genders, e.g.

7	he ðæs frofre gebad

'He lived to receive solace for that (i.e. being found as a waif).'

137	wæs to fæst on ðam

'He was too much bent on that.'

487	ahte ic holdra ðy læs,
deorre duguðe,	ðe ða dead fornam.

'I had the fewer lieges, in that death had taken those off.

1248	ge æt ham ge on herge,	ge gehwæðer ðara

'At home and in the field, both of these.'

1944	Huru ðæt onhohsnode	Hemminges mæg

'I trow H.'s son put a stop to that (i.e. her taking a man's life).'

Most of the examples of this usage are of the *he ðæt* (*ic ðæt, me ðæs*, etc.) type illustrated in the first citation.

We may now summarise the results of our investigation on one point, viz. the use in *Beowulf* of the pronoun *se ðæt* in any oblique case:

(i) It is agreed by everybody that in the group just illustrated (forty-four instances) the pronoun is the demonstrative whether the sentence in which it occurs is principal or subordinate. The pronoun is never the headword in any of these.

(ii) In another group of sentences, examined in 37, the pronoun is always the headword. These have been shown to be relative clauses according to the prose rule, and they are, in fact, indistinguishable from clauses admitted by everybody to be relative, found elsewhere in the poem; yet they are all taken by editors as principal sentences in which the pronoun is the demonstrative.

41. We shall now consider more particularly the *he ðæt* form of principal sentence, in which, as in the *he þa* form, the personal pronoun was no doubt proclitic to the demonstrative. This *he ðæt* form might be used in two ways; in the first the demonstrative, as a pronoun of general reference, looks back to the sentence before, as in

1652   Hwæt, we þe þas sælac...lustum brohton...
          Ic þæt unsofte   ealdre gedigde,

'I hardly survived that (effort, experience) with my life.'

2333   Hæfde ligdraca   leoda fæsten...
          gledum forgrunden;   him þæs guðkyning,
          Wedera þioden,   wræce leornode.

'For that (outrage) the war-king devised vengeance.'

It should be observed that this neuter demonstrative never has reference to a specific noun but only to an action or event implied in the preceding sentence. The pronoun of specific reference is always 'hit', as in

1607   wigbil wanian;   þæt wæs wundra sum,
      þæt *hit* eal gemealt   ise gelicost,

where 'hit' refers to 'wigbil';

2156   sume worde het,
      þæt ic *his* ærest ðe   est gesægde;

where 'his' refers to 'hildesceorp' in the line before;

313   [hof] getæhte,   ðæt hie *him* to mihton,

where 'him' refers to 'hof'. The reference of this pronoun is always to a noun *preceding* it, though it may, of course, be followed also by a noun in apposition, as in

1207   he (i.e. Higelac) ða frætwe wæg   ofer yða ful,
      rice ðeoden.

On the other hand, in contexts like

```
14                    fyrenðearfe ongeat,
        þe hie ær drugon       aldorlease
        lange hwile;  . him þæs Liffrea | woroldare forgeaf;
2426    Fela ic on giogoðe .    guðræsa genæs,
        orleghwila;    ic ðæt eall gemon.
```

it would be doing violence to poetic idiom (not to mention the concord rule) if we referred 'þæs' or 'þæt' to the noun, appropriate in sense though it may be, in the preceding sentence instead of to the more general thought 'their having suffered distress without a leader', 'my surviving many shocks of battle'.

42. In its second use the demonstrative pronoun is proleptic, i.e. it points forward to a noun-clause, which may be either a dependent statement or a dependent question, e.g.

```
290     Ic þæt gehyre,     þæt þis is hold weorod
277                     Ic þæs Hroðgar mæg
        þurh rumne sefan˙    ræd gelæran,
        hu he frod ond god     feond oferswyðeð—
```

In each of these the noun-clause is objective; it may equally well be a subject-clause, as in

```
1463                    næs ðæt forma sið
        ðæt hit ellenweorc     æfnan scolde,
1846    gif þæt gegangeð,     þæt ðe gar nymeð,
```

where again the first þæt is proleptic to the clause following. There is no need to illustrate this very common use further.

43. Was ðæt ever proleptic, not to a noun-clause, but to a noun? There are three places in Beowulf where it is usually taken to be so; one of them may be at once dismissed, viz.

```
2000    Ðæt is undyrne,     dryhten Higelac,
        (micel) gemeting,     monegum fira,
        hwylc orleghwil     uncer Grendles
        wearð on ðam wange;
```

here 'micel' is a mere conjecture which cannot be right, since to make ðæt proleptic to 'gemeting' when it already has its normal proleptic reference in the dependent question 'hwylc orleghwil...'

only gives us a syntactical freak; the simplest emendation is
'on ða gemeting', the sense being (97) "'Tis known, as regards
that encounter, what manner of fight there was'. There remain the
two passages

194	Ðæt fram ham gefrægn	Higelaces ðegn
	god mid Geatum,	Grendles dæda;
3087	Ic wæs ðærinne	ond ðæt eall geondseh,
	recedes geatwa;	

In both we have a supposed reference to specific nouns which
are in the plural—a construction difficult to credit. For 194 see
101; in 3087 is not 'geatwa' the usual genitive after a neuter
'eall'? If so, the ðæt is perhaps otiose.

44. A few words may be added, in conclusion, on the forms of
the relative pronoun in *Beowulf*; see also *SS* Cap. XII. In OE
prose the relative pronoun in a limiting clause was normally ðe,
as always in *ASC*; the pleonastic form seðe occurs, however,
occasionally (*SS* 119) in late WS prose. In a descriptive clause
(*SS* 118) the pronoun was

(i) normally se (ðæs, ðæm), as in *ASC* and predominantly in
Oros. and *Bede*;

(ii) seðe (ðæs de, ðæm ðe) in *Hom.*, *LS*, *CP*, and WS *Gospels*
(in Ælfric it is common only in the nominative case);

(iii) the epanaleptic sé ðe in the *Rushworth Gospel* (*SS* 117) and
sporadically in other writings.

45. Our text of *Beowulf* shows both a mixture of types and a
syntactical licence in the use of them to which there is no parallel
in any prose work: (1) in limiting clauses there are

(i) forty-two instances of ðe, twenty-six after a noun-antecedent and sixteen after the demonstrative se;

(ii) twenty-two instances of seðe, e.g.

86   Ða se ellengæst...seðe in þystrum bad

For the false concords in this group see 67;

(iii) one certain instance of se, e.g. 2407 se...se ðæs orleges or
onstealde;

(iv) at least twenty instances of epanaleptic *sé ðe* (usually in an oblique case), e.g.

1195   healsbeaga mæst
   þára ðe ic on foldan   gefrægen hæbbe.
1577   guðræsa fela
   ðára ðe he geworhte   to West-Denum
2295   [guman] þóne ðe him on sweofote   sare geteode;

in all of which the stress on the epanaleptic demonstrative is certified by the metre.

46. (2) In descriptive clauses we have

(i) fifty-three instances of *se*, twenty-six in the nominative and twenty-seven in oblique cases, e.g.

194   Higelaces þegn...;
   Se wæs moncynnes   mægenes strengest
12   [cyning] Ðæm eafera wæs   æfter cenned.

(most of these are taken by editors as demonstratives);

(ii) twenty-eight instances of *seðe* (*ðæs ðe*, etc.), e.g.

103   mære mearcstapa,   seðe moras heold
877   wide siðas,
   þara ðe gumena bearn   gearwe ne wiston,
1298   rice randwiga,   þone ðe heo on ræste abreat,

(iii) a number of instances of the epanaleptic *sé ðe*, e.g.

3002   frean userne...þone ðe ær geheold
   wið hettendum   hord ond rice,

'Our lord, him who beforetime held the realm...';
The number is not easy to determine exactly, since some of those counted under *seðe* may well belong to this class, e.g.

230   [weard] sé ðe holmclifu   healdan scolde,

'The watchman, he whose duty was to guard the sea-cliffs.'

2257   [feormynd] þá ðe beadogriman   bywan sceoldan;

'The cleansers, they whose work it was to burnish the war-mask.'

Zupitza's facsimile, however, seems to certify *seðe*, not *se ðe*, as the MS. form almost everywhere;

(iv) in *Beowulf*, as in prose, ðe is idiomatic after personal pronouns or proper nouns, e.g.

237   Hwæt syndon ge ðe þus...cwomon,
499   [Unferð] ðe æt fotum sæt   frean Scyldinga.

So much for the mixture of types. As for grammatical irregularity, a single group may be cited by way of example, viz. that in which a genitive plural is used epanaleptically, e.g.

1407   [magoeðegna] ðara ðe mid Hroðgare   ham eahtode.

These all have a metrical, as well as a syntactical, abnormality in common, which will be discussed in 154–6.

47. Our argument in the last three chapters may be thus summarised:

(1) There are in *Beowulf* four forms of ða-sentence in which the verb is stressed, viz.

(a) The *com ða* form.
(b) The *he ða* form, e.g. he ða fag gewat.
(c) The *ða he...com* form, e.g. ða he hean gewat.
(d) The *ða com* form, e.g. ða com non dæges.

Of these, (a) with a noun as subject (if expressed), and (b) with a pronoun-subject are principal sentences and take the place of the prose *ða com* form (12); (c) and (d) are subordinate clauses (3–8). We have thus a well-balanced group of four distinct forms, each with its special function. The four editions make all four forms interchangeable as principal sentences: to which the objections are (i) that such a complete confusion of types is not credible; (ii) that the limiting of subordination to clauses which follow a principal sentence is repugnant to all linguistic practice (9); (iii) that the extreme rarity of *ða com* forms, if they are principal sentences, is inexplicable (11); (iv) that the scansion, especially of (c) forms in *b* verses, is often impossible except on the unwarranted assumption that the adverb *ða* could be stressed or unstressed at pleasure.

(2) Of ðær-sentences with a stressed verb there are only two forms:

(a) The *he ðær* form, e.g. ic ðær furðum cwom.
(b) The *ðær he...com* form, e.g. ðær him hel onfeng.

The first (we have argued) is found only in principal sentences, and the second only in subordinate clauses. The four editions, however, once more make them interchangeable as principal sentences; against this the objections (i), (ii) and (iv) above are equally valid.

(3) *Ða* (*ðær*) *wæs*: this ambivalent form is taken by all the editions as a principal sentence in every place but one (2372 ða wæs Hygelac dead, but cf. 467). The *ðær wæs* form admits of this construction, even in *b* verses, if, but only if, it can be shown that *ðær* (adv.) might be expletive in *Beowulf* and therefore unstressed; otherwise *ðær*- and *ða*-forms alike are subject to the metrical objection stated in (iv) above (15, 24).

(4) *Se*, *ðæt*: we have argued that when the pronoun is the antecedent, as in

2406   Sé wæs on ðam ðreate   ðreotteoða secg
           se ðæs orleges   or onstealde,

it is the demonstrative, but when not the antecedent, if it is the headword as in the exx. in 35, 37, it is the relative. In all these latter, however, the editors take it as a demonstrative; the objections to this are (i) that in both groups (35 and 37) the pronoun has an obvious construction, and makes good sense, as a relative; (ii) that where the pronoun is in an oblique case as in 37, the same sentence-forms are rightly recognised elsewhere as relative clauses in all the editions; (iii) that where the pronoun is the nominative *se*, it has usually no sense except as a mere pronoun of reference (=*he*); if it can bear this weakened sense, why is it never found instead of *he* in subordinate clauses?—e.g. in 1506 Bær ða seo brimwylf ða *heo* to botme com; (iv) in both groups we again have the problem of the 3-lift *b* verse (36).

(5) The nominative *ðæt* in the sentence-form *ðæt wæs* can be either the antecedent or the relative, but it is usually a demonstrative of *general* reference.

CHAPTER V

CO-ORDINATE CLAUSES

48. In Old English as in other periods of English the subject of a co-ordinate clause, if the same as that of the principal sentence, is normally not expressed; examples from *Beowulf*, in clauses introduced by the conjunctions *ond*, *oððe*, *ac*, are

1833		þæt ic þe wel herige
	ond þe to geoce	garholt bere,
634		þæt ic eowra leoda
	willan geworhte,	oþðe on wæl crunge
562	Næs hie ðære fylle	gefean hæfdon...
	ac on mergenne	mecum wunde
	be yðlafe	uppe lægon,

By contrast, where there is a change of subject, we have

2098		swaðe weardade
	hand on Hiorte,	ond he hean ðonan
	modes geomor	meregrund gefeoll
109	ne gefeah he þære fæhðe,	ac he hine feor forwræc,

(where the two 'he's' refer to different persons). There are, here and there, exceptions to the rule among the many *ac*-clauses, e.g.

598	nymeð nydbade,	nænegum arað
	leode Deniga,	ac he lust wigeð,
2830	ðæt se widfloga...hreas on hrusan.	
	Nalles æfter lyfte...maðmæhta wlonc	
	ansyn ywde,	ac he eorðan gefeoll
2897		Lyt swigode
	niwra spella	se ðe næs gerad,
	ac he soðlice	sægde ofer ealle:

In all these the pronoun is otiose, since there is no change of subject; in 599 Kemble's 'on lust' (omitting 'he') makes good syntax and good sense, and in 2899, since 'sægde' requires an object, 'hie' (i.e. the news) is probably the right reading.

49. We have a striking illustration of this subject-rule in an *oððe*-clause in

277
```
                    Ic þæs Hroðgar mæg
  þurh rumne sefan     ræd gelæran,
  hu he frod ond god      feond oferswyðeþ—
  gyf him edwenden      æfre scolde,
  bealuwa bisigu,      bot eft cuman—,
  ond þa cearwylmas    colran wurðaþ;
  oððe a syþðan      earfoðþrage,
  þreanyd þolað,      þenden þær wunað
  on heahstede      husa selest.
```

With this, the usual, pointing, a second principal sentence (without a subject) is supposed to begin at 'oððe', meaning 'else he must endure his trouble for ever'. But this second sentence is shown by the omission of the subject to be a co-ordinate clause to 'hu he feond oferswyðeþ', a relationship which is effectively denied by the sémi-colon after 'wurðaþ;' if we remove the semi-colon and the brackets, we have a clearly articulated period. Beowulf promises to teach Hrothgar 'how he shall overcome his enemy or, failing that, go on enduring his trouble so long as his house shall stand'; the latter alternative no doubt refers to the night-watch which B. intends to keep. The 'gyf...wurðaþ' clause qualifies 'oferswyðeþ'; 'wurðan', co-ordinate to 'cuman', is a preferable reading (so Grein, cf. 1855–61), but this is immaterial to the main sentence-structure, which is the same either way.

No sense, however, can be made of the *ond*-clause in

1588
```
                    Hra wide sprong,
  syððan he æfter deaðe    drepe þrowade,
  heorosweng heardne,    ond hine þa heafde becearf.
```

where the subject can only be 'he' (=Grendel) carried on from the clause before; which makes nonsense. It is possible that 'ond' stands for the relative 'þe': 'after he had suffered the stroke that shore off his head'; in some OE texts the *ond*-sigil is a not un-common misreading of *þe*.

50. In OE prose a noteworthy exception to our rule is the negative co-ordinate clause; in the normal form of it (SS 73) the subject-pronoun is idiomatically expressed even when there is no change of subject, e.g. he ne hrymde ne he sace ne astyrede 'he cried not nor stirred up strife'. This form is sometimes found in *Beowulf* after an affirmative principal sentence, as in

857 monig oft gecwæð...ðætte selra nære...
   Ne hie huru winedrihten wiht ne logon,

where it appears to have the special shade of meaning often found in prose: 'many said that there was no better man than Beowulf, without, however, belittling their own liege-lord'.

A rarer form in prose is (ii) the clause without the subject-pronoun, and this is the regular one in *Beowulf* wherever the principal sentence is itself negative, e.g.

168 no he þone gifstol gretan moste,
   maððum for Metode, *ne* his myne wisse.

The *no* instead of *ne* in the co-ordinate clause is strange in

541   No he wiht fram me.
   fleotan meahte; *no* ic fram him wolde.
972   no ðær ænige swaðeah
   feasceaft guma frofre gebohte;
   no ðy leng leofað laðgeteona,

but the two words were often confused by scribes: see, for example, *Soul's Address* 33 in 167.

In a principal sentence the negative verb stands first, as in prose, but in a few places the subject-noun precedes it, e.g. 50 men ne cunnon, 2673 byrne ne meahte.

51. *The Asyndetic Co-ordinate clause.* We now come to an idiom which is peculiar to verse, viz. that in the co-ordinate *ond*-clause the conjunction is normally omitted. Examples of such asyndetic clauses, both principal and subordinate, are

356 Hwearf ða hrædlice þær Hroðgar sæt...;
   eode, ellenrof, þæt he for eaxlum gestod

'He turned quickly to where H. sat [and] went and stood, gallant man, at his shoulder':

891   þæt hit on wealle ætstod,
   dryhtlic iren; draca morðre swealt.

'So that the sword stood fast in the wall [and] the dragon died violently.' In the last example each of the two clauses has its own subject; in the first, where the subject is the same, it is idiomatically unexpressed in the co-ordinate clause. And so in

```
622                    sæl alamp,
          þæt hio Beowulfe...medoful ætbær;
          grette Geata leod,
```

'Time came when she brought the mead-cup to Beowulf [and] greeted the Geatish lord.'

```
1318      þæt he þone wisan      wordum nægde
               ...,             frægn gif him wære
          æfter neodlaðum       niht getæse.
```

'till he greeted the wise prince [and] asked him if he had had a peaceful night.'

```
2369      þær him Hygd gebead  '   hord ond rice,
          beagas ond bregostol;     bearne ne truwode,
```

'where H. offered him the treasure and the Kingdom [and] trusted not her son...;' in all the editions such clauses are pointed off as *principal* sentences without subject.

There are therefore two rules to be borne in mind regarding the co-ordinate *ond*-clause in verse, viz.

(i) that it is normally asyndetic;
(ii) that the subject, if unchanged, is not expressed.

52. Let us for a moment pay attention to the last example above; it is a form of the negative co-ordinate clause confined to verse and there used only after an affirmative sentence. Other instances are

```
152       Grendel...heteniðas wæg,
          singale sæce;     sibbe ne wolde | wið manna hwone
```

'waged ceaseless strife [and] would no peace with any man',

```
600       swefeð ond sendeð,     secce ne weneð...
```

'kills and devours [and] expects not resistance',

```
2463      Wedra helm...heortan sorge
          weallinde wæg;     wihte ne meahte | gebetan
```

'bore a heart swelling with grief [and] might no whit avenge...', and so also 1993, 2464, 2476, 2489, 2953, 3067.

None of these clauses can be mistaken either (i) for principal sentences, which must have a subject and in which the negative verb normally stands first, or (ii) for the co-ordinate negative clauses mentioned in 50 ii in which the conjunction *ne* stands first; they are, in fact, the negative form of the asyndetic *ond*-clause, *ne* being the negative particle, and we cannot be in any doubt that in contexts like those above or

1233	druncon win weras.	Wyrd ne cuþon,
1376		Nu is se ræd gelang
	eft æt ðe anum.	Eard git ne const,

the second sentence is a co-ordinate clause and should not be separated from the one before by more than a comma: 'men drank wine [and] knew not Fate', 'since help is again from thee alone [and] thou knowest not yet the place'. The four editions only recognise the construction in 1993 Ic sorhwylmum seað, siðe ne truwode.

On the other hand, a negative principal sentence can only be* followed by the regular negative clause (50 ii) and, for this reason, in

1929		næs hio hnah swaþeah,
	ne to gneað gifa	Geata leodum,
	maðmgestreona.	Mod Ðryðe (ne) wæg,

the better emendation in the last sentence would be 'ne mod Ðryðe wæg'; which moreover accounts for the dropping of *ne* after -na by haplography.

53. Let us now consider the two important implications of the subject-rule: (i) that the subject of a co-ordinate clause, if not expressed, is carried on from the preceding sentence. In

| 226 | sæwudu sældon,—syrcan hrysedon, |
| | guðgewædo; Gode þancedon... |

'hrysedon' is usually taken as intransitive 'their sarks rattled'; then 'syrcan' must be taken, absurdly, as the subject of 'þancedon' also. If, however, we give 'hrysedon' its usual transitive sense, we have three co-ordinate clauses with the same subject and good sense 'they made fast the sea-wood, shook their sarks, and thanked God'. Similarly in

400   sume þær bidon,
          heaðoreaf heoldon,   swa him se hearda bebead.
          Snyredon ætsomne—secg wisode—(MS. ða secg)
          under Heorotes hrof;

it is nonsense to say that 'those who remained outside hastened within'; if, however, we keep the MS. reading 'ðam (=ðā) secg wisode', we have a good subject for 'snyredon': 'some stayed outside [and] those for whom B. led the way hastened....'

665   Hæfde Kyning wuldor...
          seleweard aseted;   sundornytte beheold
          ymb aldor Dena,   eotonweard' abead.

We have a good sentence only if it means 'the Kingly Glory had set a hall-guard [and] held special charge concerning the Danish prince', but this is not the sense which the context requires; it was obviously the God-appointed Beowulf who 'held special charge', and for this we want some word like *se* (=who) before 'sundornytte'. Haplography would account for its dropping out. All the editions, while retaining the MS. reading, assume a change of subject, contrary to the rule. And so they do in

2903   him on efn ligeð   ealdorgewinna
          sexbennum seoc: sweorde ne mihte
          on ðam aglæcan...wunde gewyrcean.

where 'ealdorgewinna' (=the dragon) is certainly an impossible subject of 'mihte'. It may be said with confidence that 'sweord' is the right reading 'sword could not wound the monster'; the personification of the instrument is idiomatic in *Beowulf*, cf. 2673 byrne ne meahte geoce gefremman. Some editors assume the same unwarranted change of subject in

1808   heht his sweord niman,
          leoflic iren;—sægde him þæs leanes ðanc.

The change of *number* in the verb in

3030   Weorod eall aras;
          eodon unbliðe   under Earnanæs,

where the second sentence is a co-ordinate clause, is quite regular and indeed idiomatic (65) when the subject is a collective noun.

54. So far our examples have been co-ordinate principal sentences; let us now look at some co-ordinate dependent clauses:

```
1349                    ðæra oðer wæs....
        idese onlicnes;      oðer earmsceapen
        on weres wæstmum     wræclastas træd,
```

The second 'oðer', like the first, depends on 'ðæra' and should not be severed from it: Sweet's reading in the second line 'idese onlic, wæs oðer earmsceapen', seems to me preferable: 'of which one was like a woman, [and] the other was a misbegotten wretch [and] trod the paths of exile in the shape of a man'.

```
1435    ðæt...he on holme wæs
        sundes þe sænra,     ðe hine swylt fornam.
        Hræþe wearð on yðum     mid eoferspreotum
        hearde genearwod,
```

The full stop leaves 'wearð' without a subject; the first sentence shares its subject with the second, which should be shown to be co-ordinate to it: 'so that he was the more sluggish in swimming for the death that had taken him off [and] was quickly hemmed in with boar-spears'. In

```
323                     þa hie to sele furðum
        in hyra gryregeatwum     gangan cwomon.
        Setton sæmeðe     side scyldas...;
        bugon ða to bence...
```

'setton' is co-ordinate to 'cwomon' and 'bugon ða' is the principal sentence: 'as soon as they had reached the hall [and] set their shields, sea-weary men, by the wall, then bowed they to bench' (see 9 iii). In

```
2616                    þæt him Onela forgeaf,
        fyrdsearo fuslic,—no ymbe ða fæhðe spræc,
```

we have apparently a co-ordinate negative clause: 'which Onela gave him [and] said not a word (=without saying a word) about the feud'.

55. We must now consider the other implication of the subject-rule, viz. (ii) that if 'he' appears in the co-ordinate clause the subject must have changed; thus 'he' is correctly expressed in

746   nam ða mid handa   higeþihtigne
        rinc on ræste. . . ;   he onfeng hraþe

because the subject of 'onfeng' is no longer Grendel but Beowulf; and it is correct also in

1408   Ofereode þa   æþelinga bearn
        steap stanhliðo,   stige nearwe. . . ;
        hé feara sum   beforan gengde

but only if 'bearn' is taken as a plural (85), so that 'he' (the King) is distinguished from his escort, which is the subject of the sentence before. In

1154   Sceotend Scyldinga   to scypon feredon
        eal ingesteald. . .   Hie on sælade
        drihtlice wif   to Denum feredon,

'hie' is not the subject but the object: '[and] her, the royal lady, (we have just been told that she was captured) they conveyed to Denmark'. It is possible that in

2395   he gewræc syððan
        cealdum cearsiðum,

'he' is a misreading of 'hine', since the verb needs an object (it always has one in the poem) but not a subject: 'and avenged him thereafter in chill campaigns'. But in

2789   He ða. . .dryhten sinne   driorigne fand
        ealdres æt ende;   he hine eft ongon
        wæteres weorpan,

unless we are to suppose that the dying King sprinkled himself with water, the subject-pronoun can only be otiose and unidiomatic. And so in

886   syððan wiges heard   wyrm acwealde. . . ;
                            [he] under harne stan,
        æþelinges bearn   ana geneðde
        frecne dæde.

'When brave in battle, he killed the worm [and] alone, under the hoar rock, ventured the bold deed'; (here, and in

179   helle gemundon
        in modsefan,   Metod [hie] ne cuðon,

the scribe has perhaps placed the pronoun in the wrong clause).

2522   ac ic ðær heaðufyres   hates wene,
        oreðes ond attres;   forðon [ic] me on hafu
        bord ond byrnan.

'But here I expect hot battle-flame...[and] therefore have upon me corslet and shield (see 152).'

3160   bronda lafe...wealle beworhton.
        [Hi] on beorg dydon   beg ond siglu,

'What was left from the burning they compassed with a wall [and] laid the rings and jewels in the barrow.' All these without the bracketed pronouns become normal; in the following, however, the remedy may be different

963   Ic hine hrædlice...wriðan ðohte...;
       ic hine ne mihte,   ða Metod nolde,

'I thought to bind him speedily, *but* could not, since the Lord willed it not.'

1992   Ic ðæs modceare
        sorhwylmum seað,   siðe ne truwode
        leofes mannes;   ic ðe lange bæd

'I was tossed by surgings of grief [and] put no trust in a loved man's adventure *but* long besought thee'; in both of these the second 'ic' is perhaps a misreading of *ac*, since sense demands an adversative conjunction, and the pronoun is otiose.

56. A few words ought to be said about co-ordinate clauses, in certain contexts, which are not asyndetic but introduced, as in prose, by the conjunction *ond*. Most of these seem to be specially designed (*SS* 98) to avoid conjunctive order in the asyndetic clause, e.g.

652   Gegrette þa   guma oþerne,
       Hroðgar Beowulf,   ond him hæl abead,

particularly where there is a change of subject, as in

2447   þonne his sunu hangað
       hrefne to hroðre,   ond he him helpe ne mæg | gefremman.

Such clauses need to be carefully distinguished from those in which the pronoun is stressed rhetorically by contrast, as in

1412   Hé feara sum   beforan gengde,

'[while] hé (i.e. the King) went in advance'. The position of the stressed pronoun is as regular here, in verse or in prose, as a noun would be in the same position.

Of other ond-clauses the most common are either (i) the ond ða kind mentioned in 14, or (ii) sentences where the verb is in the imperative, e.g.

1216   Bruc ðisses beages...,   ond þisses hrægles neot,
          þeodgestreona,   ond geðeoh tela...

Polysyndeton seems to be particularly frequent in this latter kind of sentence.

57. The following is a list of the asyndetic clauses co-ordinate to principal sentences, not usually recognised in the modern editions: 118, 166, 172, 207, 226, 227, 264, 358, 402, 448, 614, 745, 827, 828, 925, 967, 1045, 1072, 1129, 1157, 1215, 1233, 1242, 1311, 1401, 1412, 1493, 1502, 1519, 1533, 1539, 1657, 1687, 1809, 1830, 1889, 1917, 1931, 1994, 2140, 2156, 2179, 2183, 2209, 2296, 2464, 2470, 2488, 2510, 2523, 2604, 2705–6, 2724, 2863, 2937, 2953, 3031, 3163, 3173.
Some of these have already been discussed in this chapter, and two other general comments may be made here: (i) in sentences like

207   fiftyna sum...sundwudu sohte,

358   eode ellenrof,   ðæt he for eaxlum gestod,

419   selfe ofersawon,   ða ic of searwum cwom,

'sum' 'ellenrof' and 'selfe' are not themselves the subjects but adjectival to the subjects which are carried on from the sentences before (95, 96); the lines cited should all be punctuated as co-ordinate clauses; (ii) the co-ordinate clause is often used in the

Inquit-formula either to define 'maðelode' or to describe an accompanying action, e.g.

2510	Beowulf maðelode, beotwordum spræc
1687	Hroðgar maðelode—hylt sceawode,
2862	Wiglaf maðelode..., —seah on unleofe—

We find, also, however

2724	Biowulf maðelode,—*he* ofer benne spræc,
925	Hroðgar maðelode,—*he* to healle geong,
	stod on stapole, geseah steapne hrof

in which the otiose pronoun and its intercepted position both arouse suspicion; we have the right form in 2510 and 1687 above, and 'he' in this context is therefore hardly credible.

58. Clauses co-ordinate to *dependent* sentences, usually unrecognised in modern editions, are the following: 14, 57, 78, 90, 97, 107, 152, 154, 325, 419, 557, 625, 823, 883, 887, 892, 895, 1137, 1200, 1258, 1351, 1377, 1437, 1468, 1567, 1642, 1684, 1742, 1755, 1820, 1898, 1959, 2061, 2160, 2165, 2281, 2319, 2321, 2370, 2393, 2395, 2430, 2446, 2451, 2476, 2482, 2618, 2693, 2717, 2832, 2919, 3043, 3067, 3131.

Many of these, again, have already been discussed, but two particular groups deserve a word of comment:

(i) Those in which the subject changes to a noun should not be mistaken for principal sentences, though they are often in form indistinguishable from them, e.g.

822	wiste ðæt his aldres wæs ende gegongen,
	dogera dægrim. Denum eallum wearð
	...willa gelumpen.

'Knowing that the end of his days was come [and] the desire of the Danes fulfilled.'

1754	ðæt se lichoma læne gedreoseð,
	fæge gefealleð: fehð oðer to,

'It befalls that the mortal body declines to its doom [and] another man seizes the heritage'; see also 107, 557, 892, 1137, 1258, 1567, 1642, 1742, 1898, 2061. In

2445		þæt his byre ride
	giong on galgan; þonne he gyd wrece,
	sarigne sang, ðonne his sunu hangað

''Tis sad to endure that his boy should ride on gallows [and that] himself should utter his dirge when his son is hanging'; the order 'ðonne he' disallows a principal sentence.

(ii) Some of those introduced by the strong negative *nealles* 'by no means' or the adversative *no ðy ær* 'yet not' should similarly not be taken as principal sentences, e.g.

2918   ðæt se byrnwiga   bugan sceolde,
            feoll on feðan: nalles frætwe geaf | dugoðe.

'So that the warrior must needs bow to his death [and] gave not treasure to his fighting men.'

2158   cwæð ðæt hyt hæfde   Hiorogar cyning...;
            no ðy ær suna sinum   syllan wolde,

'Saying that H. long possessed it [and] yet would not give it to his son', and so also 2832, 1502, 1537; except in co-ordination all these are without subject.

59. Since a sentence of the *com þa* form is a self-contained principal sentence, it seems hardly credible that it could also be used as a co-ordinate clause. Supposed instances are usually capable of a different interpretation, e.g.

743   sona hæfde
            unlifigendes   eal gefeormod,
            fet ond folma.   Forð near ætstop,
            nam þa mid handa   higeþihtigne
            rinc on ræste,

The full stop should be after 'ætstop' which is co-ordinate to 'hæfde gefeormod', and the new principal sentence begins with 'nam þa': 'in a trice he had bolted the body, hands and feet, [and] stepped forward nearer still. Then seized he in his hands the great-hearted warrior....' In one or two passages, however, where there are such *ða*-sentences in sequence, this remedy is not open to us, e.g.

115   Gewat ða neosian   syððan niht becom...
           Fand ða ðær inne   æþelinga gedriht

'Then went he to see how they had settled themselves in the hall [and] found therein a company sleeping'; here 'Fand ða' is inappropriate as a principal sentence since it does not begin as it

should, a new action, but only completes the first. Is *ða* a dittograph? In

1209   he under rande gecranc;
          gehwearf ða in Francna fæþm   feorh cyninges
1572   He æfter recede wlat,
          hwearf ða be wealle...

both word-order and sense demand a correlative *ða* in the first
clause.

60. We shall now consider some forms of true parataxis, in
which a co-ordinate clause is idiomatically used to indicate
subordination to the sentence before. Such clauses are subject to
the same two rules as other co-ordinate clauses, but they have also
a third characteristic of their own, viz. that the verb regularly
stands first in its clause. They may be classified under the same
heads as in prose (*SS* 103):

(i) Those introduced by *wolde*, equivalent to an adverbial clause
of purpose, e.g.

1546   Ofsæt ða ðone selegyst,...wolde bearn wrecan,

'Then bestrode she the stranger so as to avenge her child'; and so
664, 755, 796, 1010, 1292, 1339, 2294, 2305, 3171.

(ii) Those introduced by *wende*, *wiste*, *cwæð*, equivalent to an
adverbial clause of reason, e.g.

646   wiste ðæm ahlæcan
          to ðæm heahsele   hilde geðinged,

'knowing that battle was appointed for the monster',

198   Het him yðlidan
          godne gegyrwan;   cwæð, he guðcyning
          ofer swanrade   secean wolde,

'saying that he would seek out the King over the swan-road';
and so *wende* 1604, 2187, 2239, *wiste* 764, 821, 2339, 2725, *con cuðe*
359, 2062, *cwæð* 92, 1810, 1894, 2158, 2939, 3180.

(iii) Those performing the function of a defining clause, e.g.

1711   ne geweox he him to willan, ac to wælfealle...;
          breat bolgenmod   beodgeneatas,

'He grew not up to their liking but for his people's death, slaying
his table-companions in his anger'; and so 1319, 1996, 2389, 2981,
3166, (after *swa*) 539, 2991.

61. Some examples in these three groups require a word of comment; in

1010   wolde self cyning   symbel þicgan.

2305   wolde se laða   lige forgyldan

'self cyning', 'se laða' are perhaps not the subjects but appositive to the subjects and should be within commas. It would appear from

730   þa his mod ahlog;
        mynte þæt he gedælde...lif wið lice,

755   Hyge wæs him hinfus,   wolde on heolster fleon,

that a phrase like 'his mod' could be taken *ad sensum* as = 'he'; 'he laughed in his heart, thinking that he should part life from body'. In

359   [for eaxlum gestod];   cuðe he duguðe þeaw.

2339, 2725   wisse he gearwe,

we have the forbidden otiose 'he' in the paratactic clause: in 359 it is almost certainly a misreading of 'hī' (=him), for idiom requires the ethic dative. Cf. 2062 con him land gearwe, *Guth.* 286 cuðe him soð genog. Among defining clauses we have, apparently, examples of the proleptic *swa* not uncommon in prose, e.g.

538   ond ðæt geæfndon swa.
        Hæfdon swurd nacod,   ða wit on sund reon,

'and fulfilled our vow, holding our swords unsheathed....'

2989   him fægre gehet
        leana mid leodum,   ond gelæste swa;
        geald ðone guðræs...mid ofermaðmum,

'he made fair promise of payment, and fulfilled it by rewarding their battle-charge with exceeding treasure.'

62. It remains to mention that the paratactic sentences found in prose, which function as adjective clauses, do not occur in *Beowulf*; the verb in such clauses was usually *hatte* or *wæs*. *Hatte* is never found in the poem, the passive being used instead, e.g. 263 æþele ordfruma, Ecgðeow haten (where the prose idiom would have 'hatte'). In

100   oð ðæt an ongan
        fyrene fremman   feond on helle;
        wæs se grimma gæst   Grendel haten,
        mære mearcstapa,

it would be better to make 102 a parenthesis (see 71) and take
'mearcstapa' in apposition to 'feond'. *Wæs*-clauses are common
in the poem, but they are all adverbial, e.g.

2208   he gehold tela
        fiftig wintra—wæs ða frod cyning,—

'He ruled it well for fifty years, being then an aged King,' and so
auxiliary *hæfde* in

827   nihtweorce gefeh... Hæfde East-Denum
           Geatmecga leod   gilp gelæsted,

'rejoiced in his night-work, having made good his boast.' Other
exx. 137, 2981, 2321, 2361, 2952.

63. The right punctuation of a paratactic as of any other co-
ordinate clause, even in a dependent sentence, is a comma (*SS*
107), since any greater stop would disintegrate the syntax, e.g.

644   oþ þæt semninga
        sunu Healfdenes   secean wolde
        æfenræste;   wiste þæm ahlæcan
        to þæm heahsele   hilde geþinged,

2184   swa hyne Geata bearn   godne ne tealdon... ;
            swyðe wendon,   þæt he sleac wære,

2319   hu he hord eft gesceat,
        dryhtsele dyrnne   ær dæges hwile.
        Hæfde landwara   lige befangen,

In all these, it will be observed, the paratactic verb is attached to
a subordinate clause and cannot be severed from it without
damage.

How damaging mispunctuation can be will by this time have
become obvious to the reader. The injury which it does is twofold,
(i) by breaking up a periodic structure into a 'sequence of short,
disconnected principal sentences, and (ii) by leaving many of these
supposed principal sentences without a subject. Examples need
not be repeated from *Beowulf*, but one out of many from Milton

may be cited; disintegration would be fatal to his very similar idiom if in

> Since God is light
> And never but in unapproachèd light
> Dwelt from Eternitie, dwelt then in thee,

we substituted a colon or full stop for the comma before the last clause.

64. Co-ordinate sentences may have other words in common besides the subject; the most important of these is the object. We have an instance of the pronoun-object in

22   þæt hine on ylde   eft gewunigen
       wilgesiþas,   þonne wig cume,
       leode gelæsten;

'that his comrades may support him and his people stand by [him]'. Instances where both noun-object and pronoun-subject are carried on are

3131   dracan ec scufun,
       wyrm ofer weall-clif,   leton weg niman,

'the dragon too [they] thrust over the cliff and gave to the tide', and

418   forðan hie mægenes cræft   minne cuþon;
       selfe ofersawon,

'because they knew the power of my strength, and had seen [it] themselves'. It would seem that in

1486   þæt ic gumcystum   godne funde
       beaga bryttan,   breac þonne moste.

where the verbs govern different cases, the appropriate genitive of 'godne bryttan' must be understood after 'breac'. It should be observed that in all these examples, it is in the first sentence that the common word or phrase finds expression; both usage and grammatical probability are against its being referred back from a later clause to the first, as has sometimes been done in

2939   cwæð, he on mergenne   meces ecgum
       getan wolde,   sume on galgtreowum...

where 'sume' has been taken as the object of 'getan': this is indeed a *hysteron proteron*. The simplest correction is to add 'hie' after 'he'.

CHAPTER VI

GENERAL PROBLEMS OF THE SENTENCE

65. *Collective Noun Rule.* The collective noun-subject in *Beowulf* is regularly followed by a singular verb, e.g. 651 Werod eall aras, 2014 Werod wæs on wynne, 40 him on bearme læg maðma mænigo, 2882 Wergendra to lyt ðrong ymbe ðeoden; we have an apparent exception in

| 1626 | Eodon him þa togeanes, | Gode þancodon, |
| | ðryðlic þegna heap, | |

but not a real one, since 'heap' is not the subject, but in apposition to the unexpressed plural subject, of Eodon ða; in 1422 folc to sægon, 'folc' is plural.

When, however, a sentence with a collective noun-subject is followed by a co-ordinate clause with the same subject, the number of the verb is changed to the plural, e.g.

1237		Reced weardode
	unrim eorla,	swa hie oft ær dydon.
	Bencþelu beredon;	
1888	Cwom þa to flode	felamodigra
	hægstealdra heap;	hringnet bæron,
3030		Weorod eall aras;
	eodon unbliðe	under Earnanæs,

In 1888 Sievers' conjecture 'beran' gives us (186) a different construction (after 'cwom') which is supported by the metre, but the plural 'bæron', though not idiomatic, is unobjectionable grammatically.

So far the subject has been a collective noun; in the following it is a collective adjective, e.g. *monig, sum* or the like:

171		Monig oft gesæt
	rice to rune;	ræd eahtedon...
857		monig oft gecwæð...
	Ne hie huru winedrihten	wiht ne logon,
1510		sædeor monig
	hildetuxum	heresyrcan bræc,
	ehton aglæcan.	

where idiom supports 'aglæcan' (gen.) as the object, not the subject, of 'ehton' in the co-ordinate clause. We have a synonym for *monig* in

794   þær genehost brægd
    eorl Beowulfes ealde lafe,
    wolde freadrihtnes feorh ealgian,

where 'wolde' should certainly be in the plural, as the following clause 'þær hie meahton swa' shows. A good example of *sum* (=many a one) as subject is

1240   Beorscealca sum
    fus ond fæge fletræste gebeag.
    Setton him to heafdon hilde-randas

'Retainers a many bowed to rest [and] set their shields at their heads....'

The second sentence in all these examples should be pointed as a co-ordinate clause.

66. *False Concords.* There are in *Beowulf* some striking breaches of the ordinary concord rules: (i) *Number:*

904   Hine sorhwylmas
    lemede to lange;
1408   Ofereode þa æþelinga bearn
2164   feower mearas...last weardode,
1032   ðæt him fela laf frecne ne meahton | sceððan,
2251   þara ðe þis lif ofgeaf,
    gesawon seledream

In the last two 'gesawon' and 'meahton' are generally corrected to 'secga' and 'meahte'; 'secga' may be regarded as certain, since the imitation in *Andreas* 1655 has both the same verb (ofgifan) and the same appositive phrase. The rest cannot be explained, as the collective concord can, by reference to any single principle, and attempts to justify them individually by some kind of analogy are not convincing. Kl. suggests that 'sorhwylmas' in 904 was felt to be equal to 'sorh'; why then is it the only instance of its kind, and why are other similar compounds (e.g. Cearwylmas) always followed by the plural? H., who justifies 1408 by the front position of the verb, may be asked the same question; he refers us to *Wanderer*

92   Hwær cwom mearg, hwær cwom mago? hwær cwom maððumgyfa?
            hwær cwom symbla gesetu?

but the number of the last verb here, as in the *Beowulf* passage, can be accounted for as an echo of the other singulars in the context. In fact, all these false concords are scribal blunders which should be removed from the text; for the ðara ðe group see 154–6.

We have a singular verb, a plural participle, and no subject in

1004   ac gesecan sceal   sawlberendra,
            nyde genydde,   niðða bearna...

The original may have been 'sawlberend gehwa', i.e. 'everyone alive of the sons of men'; cf. *Soul's Address* 129 in 167, and for 'genydde' see 168.

67. (ii) *Gender*. We have false concords in 1259, 1344, 1887, 2421, 2684, the erring word in all of them being seðe, e.g.

1343   nu seo hand ligeð,
            se þe eow welhwylcra   wilna dohte.

There are five other false concords involving 'mine' or 'grimme' in 255, 418, 2799, 1234, 2136, all of which editors correct; it may fairly be asked on what principle the five seðe instances are left uncorrected? They form an obvious group, and if it could be shown that they might all be explained by the same linguistic rule (e.g. that seðe had come to be used, like ðe, as a general relative pronoun) there would be something to be said for them; though even then we should still have to decide whether we owed them to the poet or the scribe. I have suggested (*SS* 125) that the limiting relative ðe is the poet's regular usage in 1343, cited above, and also in 1259 and 2684, and that the simple excision of se makes these sentences normal; seðe (=ðe) is a late WS form.

68. (iii) *Case*. We have false concords of case in

424   ond nu wið Grendel sceal,
            wið þam aglæcan   ana gehegan

1830	Ic on Higelace wat,	
	Geata dryhten,	
1977	Gesæt þa wið sylfne	se þa sæcce genæs,
	mæg wið mæge,	
2703	wællseaxe gebræd	
	biter ond beaduscearp,	

These are variously treated by editors; W-Ch. and Kl. correct none of them, H. and S. emend 1830 (Higelac) and 2703 (-seax). Now in 1830 there can be no doubt that the accusative, not the dative (see 97), is the right case after *on* in the sense here required, and with 'Higelac' the appositive 'dryhten' makes a good concord; H. reads 'Higelac' on metrical grounds. Kl. cites 1830 in defence of the false concord in 2703, which he retains uncorrected; since this defence now fails, 2703 can only be supported on other grounds. It is true that 'gebræd' takes the dative as often as the accusative in *Beowulf*, and, if this were all, the scales would be equally balanced for and against 'seaxe'; but the adjectives 'biter ond beaduscearp' weight the scales decisively against 'seaxe' and in favour of 'seax'. There remain 424 and 1977, as to which it may be observed that there are indications that the scribe had a predisposition (see 98) to the accusative after *wið*, since he has written 'wið rond' in 2673 and 'wið wulf' in 3027 instead of the 'ronde' and 'wulfe' which the metre demands; the alterations to 'Grendle' in 424 and 'sylfum' in 1977 are slight and similar to others in *Beowulf* accepted by most editors; cf. 'ðeodne' in 2032, 'gehwylcum' in 936.

69. *Parenthesis.* Editors vary considerably in their admission of parenthesis, and the exx. below are not from one text. Can any general principles be enunciated for the right use of it? In the first place, it seems obvious that, since the parenthesised clause is fenced off at both ends, it should be a self-contained principal sentence, e.g. (to take a quite simple instance):

1316	Gang ða æfter flore	fyrdwyrðe man
	mid his handscale	(healwudu dynede)
	þæt he þone wisan	wordum nægde...

This rule would disallow

| 423 | Wræc Wedera nið | (wean ahsodon) |

1746   (him bebeorgan ne con)
2616   (þæt him Onela forgeaf)
3115   (weaxan wonna leg)

since not one of these is a possible principal sentence; the first lacks
a subject, the second both subject and object, the fourth a finite
verb, and the third is a relative clause.

In the second place, it also seems obvious that the parenthesis
must definitely interrupt the main sentence, as in 1316 cited above,
and not stand in a possible syntactical relation to it; this condition
would disqualify the parentheses in

1493   efste mid elne   (nales andsware
              bidan wolde)
1687   Hroðgar maðelode—hylt sceawode,
1698   Ða se wisa spræc
              sunu Healfdenes   (swigedon ealle):

because the first two by the subject rule must be co-ordinate to
the principal sentences preceding them and the third is the
principal sentence itself after the temporal *ða*-clause.

70. It is not always easy, however, to decide whether a parenthesis gives the most appropriate punctuation, e.g. in

229   Ða of wealle geseah   weard Scildinga,
                       . . . hine fyrwyt bræc
              modgehygdum   hwæt þa men wæron.
              Gewat him þa to waroðe   wicge ridan.

With this punctuation we must take 'hine fyrwyt bræc' as
principal sentence to the *ða*-clause before it; but elsewhere,
e.g. 1985, it is possible to take 'hyne fyrwyt bræc' as a
parenthesis (two editors do so), and 'hine . . . wæron' may be so
taken here, in which case 'Gewat him þa . . .' is the principal
sentence. In

18   Beowulf wæs breme   (blæd wide sprang)
            Scyldes eafera

it is very doubtful whether the parenthesis can bear the sense
required ('*his* fame spread far'), for in all other instances of

'blæd' it is accompanied by the possessive (þin, his, heora); and
it is certain that a parenthesis in

```
1741                         þonne se weard swefeð,
          sawele hyrde,      (bið se slæp to fæst)
          bisgum gebunden,   bona swiðe neah,
```

disrupts the syntax, since 'bið' is the common verb of the two
subjects 'slæp' and 'bona' and must surely not be fenced off from
the latter. In 18 Kemble's 'eaferan' (gen.) makes the words
after 'breme' a regular co-ordinate clause; for 1741 see 20.

71. A parenthesis seems to be necessary, as shown, in some
places where none of the editions recognise it, e.g.

```
2190      Het ða eorla hleo    in gefetian
          Hreðles lafe...(næs mid Geatum ða
          sincmaððum selra    on sweordes had)
          þæt he on Biowulfes  bearm alegde
```

'Then bade he bring in H.'s heirloom (there was in those days no
better treasure in the shape of a sword) which he laid...'; the
sense shows that the antecedent of ðæt, however the gender be
explained, must be sought in the first sentence (see 37). In

```
100                    oð ðæt an ongan
          fyrene fremman      feond on helle
          (wæs se grimma gæst  Grendel haten),
          mære mearcstapa,
```

'mearcstapa' is better taken as appositive to 'feond on helle', with
the preceding line parenthetic; and parenthesis gives the better
construction also in

```
1455      Næs þæt þonne mætost    mægenfultuma
          þæt him on ðearfe lah   ðyle Hroðgares
          (wæs ðæm hæftmece        Hrunting nama),
          þæt wæs an foran        ealdgestreona
```

whether the last line be taken as a second relative clause (see 35)
or a principal sentence. The parenthesis in the two last exx. is the
equivalent of the paratactic 'hatte' in prose.

72. It seems to be a necessary corollary of the second rule that
the parenthesis should not interrupt the main sentence unduly,
i.e. to the extent of causing the hearers to lose the thread of it.

Most of the obvious parentheses are short—a half line or two half lines, e.g. 2778 ecg wæs iren, 55 fæder ellor hwearf aldor of earde, 835 þær wæs eal geador | Grendles grape; the longest seems to be in the 'long' lines

2994	sealde hiora gehwæðrum	hund þusenda
	landes ond locenra beaga	(ne ðorfte him ða lean oðwitan
	mon on middangearde,	siððan hie ða mærða geslogon)
	ond ða Iofore forgeaf	angan dohtor...

where the *ond ða* clause must be co-ordinate to the first sentence. There are still longer parentheses in some editions, among them one of twelve lines before 1585 'to ðæs þe on ræste geseah...'; but these are all more than doubtful.

73. Expletive *Ðær*. The expletive use of *þær*, in which the adverb is unstressed (as in ModE There lived a wife at Usher's well), appears to be a late prosaism in Old English; instances are exceedingly rare in *ASC* or *Bede*, but they are abundant in Ælfric, from whom some exx. may be given to illustrate their variety:

(i) (the simplest form) þær wæs on þære tide sum man Johannes haten;

(ii) (in both clauses) *Hom.* I. 22. 23 þa wæron þær swa fela gereorda swa þær manna wæron;

(iii) (neg. of *þær wæs*, also in both clauses) *Hom.* I. 176. 7 þær næs nan geþafung forðam þær næs nan lustfulling;

(iv) (with stressed verb) *Hom.* I. 590 ft. þær com þa micel menigu to ðam cwearterne;

(v) *Hom.* II. 504 ft. Ða comon þær fleogende twegen fægre englas.

In (iv) *ðær* is proclitic, and in (v) enclitic, to the verb; the reader will observe that *ðær nis*, not *nis ðær*, is the negative of expletive *ðær is* and, further, that in all the principal sentences the adverb comes next to the verb.

We have now to enquire whether expletive *þær* is found in *Beowulf*. Some instances at first sight appear indubitable, e.g.

284	þreanyd þolað,	þenden þær wunað
	on heahstede	husa selest.
847	Ðær wæs on blode	brim weallende,

but in both these lines scansion, and in 284 the alliteration, demands a stress on þær, which disallows it as an expletive. On the other hand, in *b* verses like 36 þær wæs maðma fela, 89 þær wæs hearpan sweg, since metre certifies unstressed þær (for otherwise we get a 3-lift verse), it may be held that we have certain instances of the expletive; this, however, by no means follows, for þær may be the relative adverb (unstressed) and this construction gives good sense in every case (see 24). Let us therefore enquire whether the expletive appears in *Beowulf* in those other contexts, as shown by the Ælfric exx. above, in which it is usual in prose:

(i) of the negative form þær næs there is no instance;

(ii) (þa wæs þær form): we have sentences like 2472 þa wæs synn ond sacu, 2982 þa wæron monige, but again the common late prose form, e.g. 'þa wæs þær synn ond sacu' 'þa wæron þær monige', never occurs;

(iii) (þa com þær form, in which the verb is stressed): if 'þa com' is always a principal sentence, as editors construe it, we might have expected 'þa com þær' in some of them, but once more we do not find it; we have indeed 'þa þær' in

331		Ða þær wlonc hæleð
	oretmecgas	æfter æþelum frægn:
1280		Ða þær sona wearð
	edhwyrft eorlum,	

which some editors take as principal sentences (making ðær expletive), but the order is against this; the right order for the expletive would be Ða frægn þær wlonc hæleð;

(iv) (þær com þa form): since com þa sentences abound in *Beowulf*, at least one example with the proclitic expletive should surely have been forthcoming, but there is not a single one.

74. It may perhaps be pleaded that the poet had his own idiom in this expletive construction. Let us, therefore, examine some of the examples cited in the various Glossaries:

271		ne sceal þær dyrne sum
	wesan, þæs ic wene.	
440		þær gelyfan sceal
	Dryhtnes dome	seþe hine deað nimeð.

972   no þær ænige swa þeah
          feasceaft guma   frofre gebohte;
1123   þara ðe þær guð fornam
2198   oðrum swiðor
          side rice   þam ðær selra wæs.
2458   nis þær hearpan sweg,
          gomen in geardum,   swylce ðær iu wæron.
3011   ac ðær is maðma hord,
          gold unrime   grimme geceapod,

The position of *ðær* in all the principal sentences except 271 and
3011 is against the expletive; in 2458 'nis ðær' is the stressed
form and 'ðær' refers to 'on his suna bure' just before, as the
parallel phrase 'in geardum' shows. Among the dependent
clauses, expletive *ðær* in 2199 does not appear to me to bear a
meaning, but 2459 seems a clear instance of it. We are, therefore,
left with at most three possible instances of the expletive, of which
it may be observed that two, 271 and 3011, are against the poet's
regular usage, cf. 3010 ne scel anes hwæt meltan, 1300 ac wæs oðer
in ær geteohhod. And we do not know whether we owe even these
three to the poet or the scribe; in fact, the evidence is against the
use of expletive *ðær*.

75. *Omission of subject.* The omission of the subject in supposed
principal sentences in *Beowulf* is almost entirely accounted for if
we make them co-ordinate clauses in which, as we saw in the last
Cap., omission of 'he' may be idiomatic. In this section we shall
confine our attention to the omission of the subject in a *subordinate*
clause. In such clauses 'he' is the normal pronoun of reference
to a noun in the principal sentence, as in

1471   ne wæs þæm oðrum swa,
          syððan he hine to guðe   gegyred hæfde.

where 'he' refers to 'þæm oðrum'. Can this pronoun of reference
be unexpressed? The problem was dealt with by Pogatscher in
Anglia, XXIII; he there describes a classification by Kraus of the
kinds of sentence in which omission is actually found, but he
admits that the classification has no scientific basis and states his
own conclusion that the pronoun-subject may be left unexpressed
where it is present to, or 'hovers' before, the hearer's mind. It is

remarkable that Pogatscher does not attempt any estimate of the comparative frequency of this departure from what he admits to be normal usage.

76. Let us therefore consider the figures for various kinds of subordinate clause in *Beowulf* in which 'he' is wanting where it would normally be expressed:

(i) in *siððan*-clauses, six out of twenty-six, viz.

6	syððan ærest wearð
	feasceaft funden;
850	siððan dreama leas
	in fenfreoðo feorh alegde.
886	siððan wiges heard wyrm acwealde,
1420	syððan Æscheres
	on þam holmclife hafelan metton
1947	syððan ærest wearð
	gyfen goldhroden geongum cempan,
1978	syððan mandryhten
	þurh hleoðorcwyde holdne gegrette,

(ii) in *þenden*-clauses, two out of eight, viz.

57	heold þenden lifde
	gamol ond guðreouw glæde Scyldingas
2418	þenden hælo abead heorðgeneatum,
	goldwine Geata.

(iii) in *þær*-clauses, two out of twenty-seven, viz.

286	Weard maðelode, þær on wicge sæt,
	ombeht unforht;
1923	þær æt ham wunað
	selfa mid gesiðum.

(iv) in *þæt*-clauses, four out of thirty-nine, viz.

68	þæt healreced hatan wolde,
300	þæt þone hilderæs hal gedigeð.
567	þæt syððan na...
	lade ne letton,
1366	no þæs frod leofað
	gumena bearna, þæt þone grund wite.

In these four groups, therefore, the percentage of omissions is exactly fourteen; if, however, we took in the figures for other kinds of clause, e.g. *ða* none out of thirty-four, *swa* one (possibly) out of thirty-seven, *gif* none out of nineteen, *nu* one out of seven, the general percentage would be nearly halved.

77. The omissions in any of the groups do not appear, even from Pogatscher's point of view, to be subject to any discoverable rational principle. Why, for example, should the subject be un-expressed in the *siððan*-clause 1947 and expressed in the next line but one

1949   syððan hio Offan flet
          siðe gesohte,

where, by Pogatscher's 'hovering' rule, one would have expected the converse if the omission was intended? And why should it be omitted in 57 and expressed in a similar clause with this verb elsewhere? In both the *þær*-clauses and one of the *þæt*-clauses (300), but in no others, Sievers attributed the omission to the scribe and restored the pronoun, and he has been followed by some editors. Assuming scribal error, do any of the usual sources of such error account for the omission? In a few cases haplography may have been the cause, e.g. in 68 before 'healreced'; but in most of them the likeliest explanation is that an appositive noun or an adjective in the clause was taken as the subject, e.g. 'ombeht' in 286, 'goldwine' in 2418, 'selfa' in 1923, and even 'mandryhten' 'feosceaft' 'gamol' 'goldhroden' in 1978, 6, 57, 1947. It would, of course, be a signal violation of poetic idiom to make, e.g. 'ombeht' in 286 the grammatical subject when it refers to the same person as 'weard' in the principal sentence; but a scribe unaccustomed to poetic usage may be excused for not knowing that.

78. *Omission of Object.* This is an appropriate place to say something about the omission of the object. We have already examined (64) cases in which the object is idiomatically omitted in a co-ordinate clause; let us now consider some instances to which this explanation does not apply:

386   Beo ðu on ofeste,   hat in gan(gan)
          seon sibbegedriht   samod ætgædere;

The order of words suggests the sense 'Bid [them all, i.e. Beowulf's men] enter and see the band of kinsmen'. The ellipsis, however, is harsh, since Beowulf's company has not been mentioned in the speech. The alternative is 'Bid the company (i.e. Beowulf's) enter and see [me]'; the order of words is awkward for this sense, and the ellipsis little less harsh. It seems better to suppose, with Bright, that the scribe, thinking of the usual infinitive of purpose after *gangan*, was misled into writing 'seon' instead of 'seo' (def. art.), with which the construction is quite simple.

442. Wen ic ðæt he wille..Geotena leode
    etan unforhte, swa he oft dyde,
    mægen Hreðmanna.

Sense demands a transitive use of 'dyde' (=æt) as in

1828 swa ðec hetende hwilum dydon (=þywdon),

and 'mægen Hreðmanna', however interpreted, should provide an appropriate object for 'dyde', i.e. an equivalent to 'Danes'.

748   he onfeng hraþe
    inwitþancum ond wið earm gesæt.

The difficulty here is twofold, the omission of an object to 'onfeng' and the inappropriateness of 'inwitþancum' (=malicious cunning) as applied to Beowulf. Cosijn's simple emendation 'inwitþanclum' meets both difficulties: 'he received the malicious schemer that instant...'. For the use of the strong adjective as a noun see 86. In

2208   he geheold tela

2939 cwæð, he on mergenne meces ecgum
    getan wolde,

the poet's usage elsewhere demands object-pronouns; H. changes 'he' in 2939 to 'hie', with the loss of the subject-pronoun (34) which is equally necessary.

2395   he gewræc syððan
    cealdum cearsiðum,

2897   Lyt swigode
    niwra spella se ðe næs gerad,
    ac he soðlice sægde ofer ealle:

have been already discussed (55, 48) in the last chapter; 2395 is
the only instance of 'gewrecan', and 2897 the only certain instance of 'secgan', without object in *Beowulf*.

79. *Apposition and Asyndeton.* When two nouns or adjectives
stand together without conjunction, the second is usually appositive to the first and, in sense, a mere variant of it, as in

993   þe þæt winreced,
           gestsele gyredon.
1641   frome fyrdhwate.

If, however, the nouns or adjectives are quite distinct in sense,
they are usually connected by *ond*, as in 40 billum ond byrnum,
33 isig ond utfus; but asyndeton, especially with nouns, is not
uncommon, e.g.

1290   helm ne gemunde,
           byrnan side,
2986   nam on Ongenðio   irenbyrnan,
           heard swyrd hilted,   ond his helm somod;

Here the first two are in asyndeton and the second two linked;
but in

1199   Brosinga mene,
           sigle ond sincfæt,

'sigle ond sincfæt,' taken together, are probably appositive to
'mene'. With adjectives of distinct sense asyndeton is rarer, but
it is found in 2025 geong goldhroden, 2950 frod felageomor, and
perhaps in 322 guðbyrne scan heard hondlocen, though here the
'heard' is more probably quasi-adverbial. Schücking's rule therefore (cited in W.-Ch.'s note on 1546) that *ond* cannot be omitted
when adjectives signify distinct qualities is by no means absolute.

80. The converse of this rule, viz. that words of the same
meaning should not be connected by a conjunction, ought to be
true and generally is, but there are two striking exceptions:

1453   þæt hine syððan no
           brond ne beadomecas   bitan ne meahton.
2659   urum sceal sweord ond helm,
           byrne ond beaduscrud   bam gemæne.

Here 'brodne' or 'brogdne' (=brandished) and 'bord' (for 'byrne') have been proposed, and by some editors accepted. It is certainly remarkable that the 'all-iron shield' specially made for Beowulf and which moreover saves Wiglaf just afterwards from the flames, should not be mentioned in 2659.

The linking of two synonymous, or nearly synonymous, words in the figure called hendiadys, is confined in *Beowulf* to verbs, e.g. 1337 wanode ond wyrde, 2430 heold mec ond hæfde.

81. Normally, an appositive noun is the same in kind (abstract, concrete, or the like) as the one to which it is in apposition; and in

875   þæt he fram Sigemunde   secgan hyrde,
        ellendædum,

3066   þa he biorges weard
        sohte searoniðas;

the emendation to 'Sigemundes' and 'searoniða' (adv. gen.), has been made for this reason; in

1462   se ðe gryresiðas   gegan dorste,
        folcstede fara;

the same rule calls for 'gryresiða'; and in

2943   syððan hie Hygelaces   horn ond byman,
        gealdor ongeaton

if 'byman' is taken as a genitive (so Schücking) it ought to carry with it 'horna' as a genitive. Again in

2212   seðe on heaum hæþe   hord beweotode,
        stanbeorh steapne;   stig under læg
                ...ðær on innan giong nathwylc

since the situation of the hoard is usually described by an adverbial phrase (cf. 2744 hord under harne stan), it is better both for this reason and for the sense of what follows to begin a new period with 'Stanbeorh' which is the antecedent of 'ðær on innan'; 'There lay a pathway beneath a lofty barrow, whereinto went some man...'.

It is possible that there lies a concealed apposition in

642   Ða wæs eft swa ær   inne on healle
        þryðword sprecen,   ðeod on sælum,
        sigefolca sweg;

the awkwardness of this sentence as it stands has been generally felt; it has three clauses with a common verb *wæs*, in the first of which *wæs* is auxiliary to the past participle, in the second it has an adverb complement, and in the third it is used absolutely; if we write 'ðeoda' in the second line the structure is perfectly simple 'then was uttered once more the proud speech of a glad people, the clamour of the victor-folk': 'sigefolca sweg' is exactly parallel to 'ðryðword ðeoda' and in apposition to it.

82. *Dubious Sentence-forms*. There are in *Beowulf* a number of principal sentences in which the subject-pronoun is the headword but, instead of being followed immediately by the verb, is intercepted from it by other words. This kind of interception is the rule both in prose and verse when the intercepting word is an adverb or a certain kind of adjective, e.g. *ða, ðær, ana*; and it is also normal in verse (i) when the subject-pronoun is stressed (130) as in 318 íc to sæ wille, 1412 hé feara sum beforan gengde, (ii) when the subject-pronoun, though itself unstressed, is proclitic to another which is stressed (131) as in 426 ic þé nu ða biddan wille, where metre certifies the stress. Some other instances of interception are only apparent and arise from scribal error, e.g. (55) in sentences like 2724 he ofer benne spræc, where 'he' in a co-ordinate clause violates the poet's idiom. But there are yet others of a different kind which we shall now consider. A simple example is

1567   bil eal þurhwod
          fægne flæschoman;   heo on flet gecrong,

The last sentence, notwithstanding its conjunctive order, poses as a principal sentence: 'the blade went clean through her fated body; she fell to the floor'. It does not sound amiss in modern English prose, where the relation of one sentence to another is frequently left to the reader's imagination; but this is quite contrary to OE poetic idiom (31, 32), which explicitly states the relation in a consecutive clause, as indeed is shown just before in the almost identical sentence

1539   brægd ða beadwe heard,   þa he gebolgen wæs,
          feorhgeniðlan,   þæt heo on flet gebeah:

if in 1568 we insert *þæt* before 'heo', not only is the conjunctive

order justified but the sentence-structure now becomes idiomatic.
And so in

2691   heals ealne ymbefeng
                biteran banum;   he geblodegod wearð

and perhaps also in

1434   þæt him on aldre stod
              herestræl hearda;   he on holme wæs
              sundes þe sænra,

where a second *þæt* before 'he' (see exx. 32) would be idiomatic.
Similarly in

1879   dyrne langað
              born wið blode.   Him Beowulf ðanan
                              ...græsmoldan træd
2124   Noðer hy hine ne moston...bronde forbærnan
              leofne mannan;   hio ðæt lic ætbær

the conjunction *ða* seems to be demanded in both the second
clauses: 'deep longing burned within him when B. departed over
the grassy turf', 'Yet might they not burn the dear man with fire
since she had carried off the corpse' (see also 59).

83. The sentences we are considering all have this in common,
that the placing of a conjunction before them makes them normal
syntactically and also accounts for their conjunctive order. Let
us take another group, in which it is a co-ordinating conjunction
which is omitted:

80   He beot ne aleh,   beagas dælde,
1738   ac him eal worold
              wendeð on willan;   he þæt wyrse ne con

These, again, pose as principal sentences; but the position not only
of the subject-pronoun but of the negative verb also (at the *end*,
instead of the beginning, of a principal sentence) is quite abnormal.
If, however, we place the conjunction *ne* before each sentence, it
becomes a perfectly normal co-ordinate negative clause (see 50)
after an affirmative sentence; *ne* might easily be dropped by the
scribe in either place.

The most usual conjunction in co-ordinate clauses is *ond*, and we know by collation of some texts how easily it was overlooked; in

1169	Onfoh þissum fulle,	freodrihten min,
	sinces brytta!	Ðu on sælum wes,
	goldwine gumena,	ond to Geatum spræc

the abnormal front position of the pronoun and the end-position of the verb (in a command) make *ond* before 'ðu' a certain emendation, the word-order now being the regular one in an *ond*-clause; the polysyndeton need not offend, we have it again with imperatives in 1216 (see 56) and elsewhere—it was in fact idiomatic.

84. We have a different type of sentence again in

958	We þæt ellenweorc	estum miclum,
	feohtan fremedon,	
1753	Hit on endestæf	eft gelimpeð,

where the only explanation of the order in a principal sentence seems to be omission of an initial exclamatory *hwæt*. We have a very similar sentence to 958 in

| 1652 | Hwæt, we þe þas sælac, | sunu Healfdenes, |
| | leod Scyldinga, | lustum brohton, |

which, like 958, is the opening sentence of a speech, and to 1753 in

| 2248 | Hwæt, hyt ær on ðe |
| | gode begeaton; |

Since 1753 is the only place in the poem where impersonal 'gelimpan' has the subject expressed, *hit* in that passage may itself represent an original *hwæt* or its abbreviation and have taken its place. A different explanation is possible for

| 1900 | He ðæm batwearde...swurd gesealde; |

here 'ðæm' probably stands for *ða* miswritten as *ðā*, cf. 2347 ðam (=ða) sæcce ondred; the sentence is the usual *he ða* form and is correlative to 'ða wæs' just before (see 103).

There is, of course, no anomaly in lines like

| 40 | him on bearme læg | maðma mænigo |

'on his breast lay many a treasure', where 'him' is idiomatically attached as a possessive to the noun, as in prose (*SS* 57).

CHAPTER VII

SOME PARTS OF SPEECH

85. We shall deal only with certain problems of form and syntax which are important for the sense or metre, or both.

Nouns. In compounds *hilde-* is reduced to *hild-* if the second component has a short stem, e.g. hildfruma, hildlatan; in 2205 hearde hildefrecan, the shorter form should be restored. Metre, however, demands the longer form in 2723 hildesædne; this should probably be written as two words 'hilde sædne' (so Kl.). The form *-getawa* presents some problems; it occurs twice, though most editors retain it only once in the text. The still longer form, 395 guðgeatawum, suggests the possibility that the second *a* (? *u*, = open *a*) is merely a bridge-letter, as in 'beaduwe', and that *-geatwa* is the true form everywhere; it may be observed that, if the poet wants a word of the metrical pattern of 'guðgetawa', he uses 'guðgewæde' which, with its other compounds, occurs frequently in *Beowulf*.

It is clear from internal evidence that in the combination *æþelinga bearn* the latter word is always a plural (so therefore (66) in 1408 Ofereode þa æþelinga bearn); when *bearn* is singular, the formula is always 'æþelinges (ðeodnes, etc.) bearn'.

86. Strong adjectives can function as nouns in all cases both singular and plural except the nominative singular, e.g. gomelum, gomele, gomelra; the acc. sing. is rare, but there are undoubted instances, e.g. 1595 ymb godne, 1977 wið sylfne, 2576 gryrefahne sloh. The interpretation of 'heard' (=sword) in some glossaries is inadmissible and so is the taking of 'deaðfæge' as the subject in the emendation of 850 Ðeaðfæge deaf (see 111).

The weak adjective with *se* can function as a noun in all cases and numbers without exception, se goda, ðæs godan, etc.; in 2931 gomela (without *se*) is recognised as a solecism and variously emended.

87. *Cases.* The existence of a descriptive genitive in *Beowulf* is dubious, though some see examples of it in

1728   Hwilum he on lufan   læteð hworfan
            monnes modgeþonc   mæran cynnes

(taking the last two words with 'monnes') and in

2353   ond æt guðe forgrap   Grendeles mægum
            laðan cynnes:

'cynnes', in 1729, is to be construed preferably with 'lufan', or its emendation, as an objective genitive, and in 2354 it should be corrected, as it is by some editors, to 'cynne'. In

1057   Metod eallum weold
            gumena cynnes:

where 'cynnes' can hardly be a partitive genitive, 'cynne' is again suggested by lines like 913 eallum wearð manna cynne... gefægra'.

The objective genitive occurs frequently in *Beowulf*, but its extended use in

378   þa ðe gifsceattas   Geata fyredon
            þyder to þance,

which some take to mean 'gifts for the Geats', seems very doubtful; Thorpe's 'Geatū', to be construed with 'to þance', is good idiom and would hardly differ from the MS. reading in the older script.

88. There are supposed instances of a causal dative without *for* in *Beowulf* which are suspect, e.g.

809   se ðe fela æror
            modes myrðe   manna cynne
            fyrene gefremede
1733   þæt he his selfa ne mæg
            his unsnyttrum   ende geþencean

(='in his destructive mood', 'because of his folly'); in the latter some editors, following Thk., read 'for' before 'his', and in the former the syllable -ror at the end of 809 may well account for the omission, through haplography, of 'for' at the beginning of the next line. It is possible to construe 'dædum' as an instrumental case in 2466 hatian ne mihte | laðum dædum, i.e. 'by hostile act'.

Another doubtful use of the dative is as a locative in 3083 wicum wunian; elsewhere the verb is either transitive or, if intransitive, is qualified by a noun governed by a preposition, and 'wicū' here might easily be a misreading of 'wica' with open *a*.

89. A doubtful accusative is

1066   ðonne healgamen   Hroðgares scop
            mænan scolde...,

where 'healgamen' is usually construed, in a kind of loose apposition, 'as an entertainment'; that Greek construction, however, is not Old English. The simplest correction of the line is 'þonne on healgamen' (=when, by way of entertainment...); *on* might easily have dropped out after a preceding *ðon*.

90. *Adjective as Attribute.* The weak declension is the rule when an adjective is used attributively with a noun which is preceded by the article or a demonstrative or possessive, e.g. se modga mæg, þas lænan gesceaft. The strong adjective in 373 wæs his eald fæder Ecgþeo haten is questionable; the obvious imitation in *Mald.* 218

            wæs min ealda fæder   Ealdhelm haten

has the weak form.

Se, however, may be understood in this attributive construction, e.g. gamela Scylding, mæran cynnes. We might have expected that this shorter form 'mæran cynnes' would always stand for the definite adjective (=*the* famous kindred); it is used, however, for both definite and indefinite indifferently, so that we get 1307 on hreon mode (in troubled mood) and 2290 dyrnan cræfte (by secret craft) by the side of 2581 on hreoum mode, 2168 dyrnum cræfte. Only in the nominative are the forms distinct in sense, e.g. geong guma '*a* young man', geonga garwiga '*the* young warrior', 2470 swa deð endig mon 'as does *a* wealthy man'.

91. The superlative is normally accompanied in *Beowulf* by a partitive genitive, e.g. husa selest 'the best house'; the right reading in 2710 is 'siðest sigehwila (see 180). Some adjectives, however, are used in two senses, with one of which the partitive

genitive is inappropriate; e.g. *mæst* means both 'greatest' and
'most' (in quantity). We have, therefore, 78 healærna mæst 'the
greatest hall', but

1079   þær heo ær mæste heold
              worolde wynne

'where till then she had had most joy',

2181   ac he mancynnes   mæste cræfte
              ginfæstan gife heold...

where the meaning seems to be 'with most skill'; but in

   459   Gesloh þin fæder fæhðe mæste

'fæhðe' must be an error for 'fæhða' (so Kl.).

The apposition of the whole and part in

   415   me ðæt gelærdon   leode mine,
              þa selestan,

instead of the normal 'leode minre ða selestan' is unique.

92. *Verbs.* The subjunctive mood in *Beowulf* is often indistinguishable in form from the indicative; this is well illustrated in
the clauses after comparatives and superlatives. These in OE
verse had the verb normally in the subjunctive, as in

Gen. 627   wifa wlitegost ðe on woruld come
Cr. 988   þær bið wundra ma
              þonne hit ænig on mode   mæge aþencan.

The only unambiguous instance after a superlative in *Beowulf* is

2129   hreowa tornost
              þara ðe leodfruman   lange begeate,

the mood after other superlatives in 1407 eahtode, 1686 dælde, etc.,
being ambiguous. In clauses after comparatives, the mood in
Beowulf always happens to be ambiguous in form, e.g.:

    70   þonne yldo bearn   æfre gefrunon
  2571   læssan hwile...þonne his myne sohte;

for a similar subjunctive plural in -*on*, cf. 3112 þæt hie bælwudu
feorran feredon.

93. Of the tenses, the preterite indicative has often the sense of a present perfect, e.g. sægdon 'they have said (and still say)'; the sequence of tenses in

377   Ðonne sægdon þæt...þæt he þritiges
       manna mægencræft   on his mundgripe
       heaðorof hæbbe

is therefore quite regular 'since they have told us that he has the strength of thirty'. The negative form *ne bið* of the substantive verb, in its normal front position, e.g. 949 ne bið þe nænges gad, is the future tense, which is thus distinguished from the present *nis* in the same position, e.g. 1372 nis þæt heoru stow. On the other hand *ne wæs* in front position introduces a co-ordinate clause, *ne* being the conjunction, and so is distinguished from *næs*, the negative verb, though the scribe has once or twice confused them. It is noteworthy that *gewearð* is used, once only in 3061, as an auxiliary with the passive participle instead of the normal *wearð* or *wæs* which is found everywhere else (see 174).

94. *Adverbs*. The use of the noun in various oblique cases as an adverb is characteristic of Old English as of some other languages; we have, for instance, in prose the four forms *ungemet* (acc.), *ungemetes* (gen.), *ungemete* (instr.), *ungemetum* (dat. pl.). Of these *ungemetes* (*unigmetes*) and *ungemete* are found in *Beowulf*, whereas *ungemet*, the prevailing form in OE verse does not occur. The *Beowulf* forms are difficult metrically, and *ungemet* would give us a more metrical type in every place. In

·150   (wearð) ylda bearnum   undyrne cuð
        gyddum geomore

('it became known to the sons of men in songs sadly') both the position of the adverb 'geomore' and its construction are abnormal; an adverb at the end of a sentence is, as a rule, immediately preceded by a verb. Perhaps 'geomorod' (=bewailed in song), appositive to 'cuð', is the right reading, cf. 1118 geomrode gyddum.

95. *Pronouns*. As a pronoun *sum* usually means 'one', e.g. 248 eower sum 'one of you', 2301 gumena sum 'one of human kind', 271 ne sceal þær dyrne sum wesan 'nor shall *one* thing be hidden' (not 'anything', for which the right word in a negative sentence is *aht*, cf. 2314 no ðær aht cwices). By meiosis, therefore, 'sum' comes to mean 'more than one, many', e.g.

1240   Beorscealca sum
           fus ond fæge   fletræste gebeag.

'many a drinker, doomed to death, bowed him to his couch'. With the genitive of a numeral, *sum* means 'one of such a number (=with so many others)'; in this construction it can only be used in apposition to a noun or pronoun, e.g.

2401   Gewat ða twelfa sum...dryhten Geata
1412   hé feara sum   beforan gengde;

'The Geatish lord with eleven others', 'he with a few others....' A sentence like

3060   Weard ær ofsloh
           feara sumne;

cannot therefore be an instance of this construction (see **171**) as some editors take it.

96. *Self* and its weak form *selfa* are used indifferently to qualify either nouns or pronouns, e.g. 594 þu self, 920 self cyning, 29 he selfa, 3054 God sylfa; neither, however, can stand alone as a pronoun in the nominative, and sentences like 419 selfe ofersawon, 1468 selfa ne dorste, should be construed as co-ordinate clauses to the sentences before which supply their noun- or pronoun-subjects.

In oblique cases *self* may stand alone, as in 700 selfes mihtum 'by his own strength', and possibly 1977 wið sylfne.

An is normally a pronoun, *ana* always an adjective with the sense 'alone', e.g. 1714 he ana hwearf, 999 hrof ana genæs. The adjective in

144   Swa rixode...ana wið eallum

is no doubt a scribal error for 'an', cf. 2267 Swa...mænde an æfter eallum.

97. *Prepositions.* In local senses the Anglian *in* and the WS *on* are used in *Beowulf* interchangeably, e.g. 19 Scedelandum in,

2357 Freslondum on; the only instance of temporal *in* is 1 in geardagum (elsewhere 'on geardagum'). For all the figurative senses of the preposition, *on* is used invariably; it is important to distinguish some of these senses. *On* with the dative of nouns denoting persons means 'on the part of' or 'from', e.g. 609 gehyrde on Beowulfe fæstrædne geþoht; *on* with the accusative means 'as regards', e.g. 2650 God wat on mec þæt me is micle leofre. In

1830	Ic on Higelac[e] wat,
Geata dryhten...,	þæt he mec fremman wile,

('I know as regards H.') sense, syntax and metre are all against 'Higelace' and there can be no doubt that it should be corrected to 'Higelac' (see 68). Another important abstract sense of *on* with non-personal nouns is 'by way of', e.g. on fultum, on ondsware; see also 89.

98. *Mid* with the accusative is another Anglianism; in *Beowulf* it occurs always in the stock phrase 'mid [eorla] gedriht', but otherwise only twice, viz. 879 buton Fitela mid hine, 2652 mid minne goldgyfan. In the first of these the pronoun is certainly unidiomatic (cf. 1649 for eorlum ond þære idese mid) and metrically suspect, and 'hine' is probably an intruder. *Wið* in most of its senses is used with the dative or accusative indifferently; there is some reason to suppose that the scribe had a dialectal preference for the accusative since this case presents us with a short verse in 2673 bord wið rond, 3027 ðenden he wið wulf, and with a false concord in

424	ond nu wið Grendel sceal
wið þam aglæcan	ana gehegan

and possibly in 1977 gesæt þa wið sylfne...mæg wið mæge (but see 96).

99. *Conjunctions.* In all glossaries *oððe* and *ac* are recorded as sometimes = 'and'; there is no need for this interpretation since in two of the supposed instances of *oððe*, viz.

2475	oððe him Ongenðeowes	eaferan wæran
	frome fyrdhwate	
3006	oððe furður gen | eorlscipe efnde	

oððæt or *oð ðe* (which occurs in *ASC*) gives excellent sense: 'till O.'s sons were bold in warfare', 'till he achieved heroic deeds yet more' (see 102). And in

1448   ac se hwita helm   hafelan werede

the simple correction of *ac* to *eac* or *ec* gives the right conjunction. In the much-debated lines

648   siððan hie sunnan leoht   geseon meahton
            oððe nipende   niht ofer ealle

the correction of a single letter, *oðre* for *oððe*, makes syntax and sense good: 'when once they could see the sun's light darkening with another nightfall'.

The pronominal *noðer*, like its positive *ægðer*, was properly followed in OE by a pair of co-ordinating conjunctions, e.g. *ægðer ge god ge yfel* 'both good and evil', *noðer ne god ne yfel* 'neither good nor evil'. In

2124   Noðer hy hine ne moston,   syððan mergen cwom...,
            bronde forbærnan   ne on bel hladan

noðer is inappropriate if taken as bracketing the two infinitives, since these are synonymous and not, as they should be, mutually exclusive. To make *noðer*, however, a conjunction (=nor), as the glossaries do, is no less a solecism, and it is probably a misreading of *no ðy ær* 'yet might they not burn him with fire or lay him on the pyre'. This adversative conjunction ('none the more', 'yet not') seems not to occur outside *Beowulf*, which may account for its being miswritten by the scribe; besides *noðer* we have the false form *no ðær* (which must be co-ordinate to *no ðy leng*) in

972   no ðær ænige swaðeah
       feasceaft guma   frofre gebohte;
       no ðy leng leofað   laðgeteona

'none the more (i.e. because of his escape) has the wretch won any comfort, none the longer shall he live'; and so perhaps in 1907.

In

1248   ge æt ham ge on herge,   ge gehwæðer ðara,

we have probably a variety of the *ægðer* formula, in which *gehwæðer* (= *ægðer*) stands after instead of before the co-ordinating conjunctions 'at home and on the field, both of these'; if so, the meaningless third *ge* is better away, being a mere dittograph of the first syllable of *gehwæðer* or the last one of *herge*. The prose form of the sentence would be '*ægðer ge æt ham ge on herge*'.

CHAPTER VIII

THE POET AND HIS ART

100. The impression made upon us by the style of a poet depends both on the quality of his linguistic instrument and on the skill with which he uses it. The resources of the language in which *Beowulf* is written are rich and varied, alike in vocabulary and in syntactical forms. Sentences and clauses especially have a variety which contrasts strikingly (see *SS* 108) with the poverty in this respect of OE prose even of the tenth century. Of temporal clauses, for example, which are the essential tissue of a vigorous narrative style, there is a particular abundance, and every temporal conjunction—*ða, ðonne, siððan, ða furðum* (=simul ac), *ðenden, nu, oððæt*—is used with an ease and precision not excelled and scarcely equalled by the mature prose of Ælfric.

101. It will be interesting to see how the poet used this group of clauses in one particular context. The main 'transitions' of his story, marking a fresh stage in the action and often a change of scene as well, are usually periodic sentences with a certain elaboration of structure and style; let us examine some different patterns in these transitions:

(i) *The first visit of Grendel*

<pre>
99   Swa ða drihtguman   dreamum lifdon
      eadiglice   oð ðæt an ongan
      fyrene fremman,   feond on helle
      (wæs se grimma gæst   Grendel haten),
      mære mearcstapa   se ðe moras heold,
      fen ond fæsten;
</pre>

'So those warriors lived in joy and happiness, till a hellish fiend (Grendel was the grim spirit's name) began to work evil, the notorious march-stepper who held the moors, the fen and the fastness.' The passage opens with a *principal swa*-sentence which looks back to what goes before and is indeed a mere résumé of it;

it is the subordinate *oððæt*-clause which now carries forward the action to a new stage. We have a similar transition in

2397   Swa he niða gehwane   genesen hæfde...,
        ellenweorca,   oð ðone anne dæg
        ðe he wið ðam wyrme   gewegan sceolde

which introduces Beowulf's first visit to the dragon's haunt, and others in 2115 and 2278 preluding the attack by Grendel's mother and the awakening of the dragon's wrath.

We have also a possible instance of the type in

194   Ðæt fram ham gefrægn   Higelaces ðegn,
        god mid Geatum,   Grendles dæda,
        ...Het him yðlidan | gegyrwan

where '*ðæt*' as a demonstrative is disallowed both by syntax (37) and by metre (163), and as a relative (with 'gewin' as antecedent) has a bad apposition in 'Grendles dæda'. The first arrival of the hero in Denmark is a great moment in the story, and we should expect it to be announced in one of the standard transitions. Now the above passage is preceded by the lines

        Swa ða mælceare   maga Healfdenes
        singala seað,   ne mihte snotor hæleð
        wean onwendan;   wæs ðæt gewin to swyð,

and assuming the usual '*oððæt*' in 194 in place of '*ðæt*' the syntax becomes straightforward, with 'dæda' as direct object of 'gefrægn' and 'het' (note the omission of subject) as the verb in a co-ordinate clause: 'So H. brooded continually on his trouble and could find no relief...until B. in his far-off home heard of Grendel's doings [and] bade prepare a goodly ship'. 'Wæs— mæst' (191–3) is a parenthesis.

It can be said with confidence that we have another instance in

544   Ða wit ætsomne   on sæ wæron
        fif nihta fyrst,   oððæt unc flod todraf....

Here the resumptive adverb *swa* ('so we were together') is demanded by idiom in place of the misleading *ða*, since the two men's adventures while swimming together have been already described at length in the lines before; the *oððæt*-clause now tells us what happened after these five days.

102. There is, however, a variety of this type which properly opens with a *ða-* instead of a *swa-*sentence, as in

(ii) *The journey to the mere*

1408   Ofereode (? -on) ða   æþelinga bearn
            steap stanhliðo,   stige nearwe...,
            he feara sum   beforan gengde...
            oððæt he færinga   fyrgenbeamas
            ofer harne stan   hleonian funde

where the two principal sentences, though carrying the narrative forward, only do so in general terms, and it is again the *oððæt-*clause which marks the crucial stage of the action: 'Then went the sons of aethelings over steep stony slopes, while he, the King, with a few others strode ahead till suddenly he came upon mountain-trees leaning over hoar-grey rock.' If the reader will compare this with

2472   Ða wæs synn ond sacu   Sweona ond Geata...
            oððe him Ongenðeowes   eaferan wæran
            frome, fyrdhwate

he will, I believe, be convinced that *oððe* (see 99) stands for *oððæt* and that the passage is a typical example of the form we are now considering. Other examples are 53 and 642, the second of which leads up to Beowulf's watch for Grendel on his first night at Hart.

103. We shall now consider a different type of transition-period in which it is a subordinate *ða-*clause which stands first.

(iii) *Finn composes the quarrel*

This is the second stage of the Finn episode, in which Finn appears on the scene for the first time and tries to heal the murderous feud between the two groups of his followers:

1095   Ða hie getruwedon   on twa healfa
            fæste frioðuwære,   Fin Hengeste
            elne unflitme   aðum benemde
            þæt he ða wealafe   weotena dome
            arum heolde   þæt ðær ænig mon
            wordum ne worcum   wære ne bræce...

'When they (the Jutes and the Half-Danes) had plighted on either side a firm peace-troth, Finn bound himself to Hengest by oaths to hold in honour the sorry remnant under the ruling of his council, upon the terms that no man there should break the agreement by word or deed....' Here the first clause is unambiguously subordinate; it carries us back to the sentence before in which the overtures between the combatants are described, and it is now the following principal sentence which advances the action a further stage. Similar examples are 662 (see 6) and the correlated sentences, 1644 and 2752, discussed in 16.

Others of the same type begin with the ambivalent *ða wæs*, where these words introduce a subordinate clause, e.g.

(iv) *Beowulf's homegoing*

1896	Ða wæs on sande	sægeap naca
	hladen herewædum,	hringedstefna
	mearum ond maðmum,	mæst hlifade
	ofer Hroðgares	hordgestreonum,
	he þa[m] batwearde	bunden golde
	swurd gesealde,	þæt he syððan wæs
	on meodubence	maðme þy weorþra...

'When the spacious ship on the sand was laden with war-gear, the ring-prowed vessel with horses and treasure, [and] the mast towered high over H.'s hoard-gifts, then gave he to the boat-ward a sword mounted with gold, such that thereafter on the mead-bench he was honoured the more because of the gifts; [and] at once the ship sailed.' Similarly the *ða*-clause in 3134 *sqq.* describes the events (see 16) before Beowulf's funeral rites, and thus brings us to the last scene of all; for the reading *ða* see 173.

104. The examples hitherto have all begun with an *a* verse; this is the rule for transitions introducing the main divisions of the poem. There are, however, within the major actions, many *minor* transitions, which usually begin with a *b* verse; a few examples of *ða*-clauses in this position will suffice:

461		ða hine Wedera cyn
	for herebrogan	habban ne mihte,
	þanon he gesohte	Suðdena folc...

'When the Weder-kin could not hold him for fear of war, thence sought he the South-Dane folk...'

518   ða hine on morgentid
        on Heaðo-Ræmas   holm up ætbær,
        þonon he gesohte   swæsne eþel...

'When at morning-tide the flood cast him up in the land of the Heathoremes, thence sought he his own loved home.' In some we have an unmistakable correlation:

323   þa hie to sele furðum
        in hyra gryregeatwum   gangan cwomon,...
        bugon þa to bence;

'So soon as they reached the hall, they bowed them then to the bench.'

1008   Ða wæs sæl ond mæl
        þæt to healle gang   Healfdenes sunu...,
        ne gefrægn ic þa mægðe   maran weorode
        ymb hyra sincgyfan   sel gebæran.

'When 'twas time and the hour that H.'s son should go to hall, never heard I of a people that with greater company bore them better about their treasure-giver.'

In all the above *ða*-clauses the *ða* is shown by scansion to be unstressed and must, therefore, be a conjunction, but in

1151   Ða wæs heal roden
        feonda feorum,   swilce Fin slægen...,
        sceotend Scyldinga   to scypon feredon
        eal ingesteald...

and elsewhere, syntax and metre alike tolerate *ða wæs* either as a principal or a dependent sentence; yet the poet's usage undoubtedly gives preference to its construction as a subordinate clause, whenever, as here, it yields as good sense (see further 118).

The *ða*-clauses cited' in the last two sections are, without exception, punctuated as principal sentences in the four editions.

105. The reader will have observed that almost all the transitions so far, produce on the mind by their backward reference an effect of retardation; and he may ask whether the poet has no

means of conveying the contrary impression of rapidity. He does so, both in major and minor transitions, by the simple device of a *sequence* of short asyndetic principal sentences, e.g.

320	Stræt wæs stanfah,	stig wisode
	gumum ætgædere,	guðbyrne scan
	heard hondlocen,	hringiren scir
	song in searwum...	
1159		Leoð wæs asungen,
	gleomannes gyd,	gamen eft astah,
	beorhtode bencsweg,	byrelas sealdon
	win of wunderfatum...	
1569	sweord wæs swatig,	secg weorce gefeh.
	Lixte se leoma,	leoht inne stod...

In the last the new paragraph should begin with 'sweord wæs swatig', which is the first sentence of a sequence.

Single short sentences, however, especially half lines, are avoided except in gnomic judgements (to be dealt with presently) or parentheses. Exceptions like

136	ond no mearn fore;	wæs to fæst on þam.
891		þæt hit on wealle ætstod,
	dryhtlic iren;	draca morðre swealt.

are only apparent, the second clause being really co-ordinate to the one before (51, 62). And in

1649	...egeslic for eorlum	ond þære idese mid
	wliteseon wrætlic;	weras onsawon.

it is better to make 'wliteseon' object of 'onsawon' with a comma after 'mid', cf. 1440; 1422 folc to sægon, usually cited in support of this text, is a parenthesis.

106. *Speeches.* Considerably more than a third of *Beowulf* consists of speeches, which have some features peculiar to themselves. They are frequently introduced by an *inquit*-formula which consists of the verb *maðelode*, a proper noun, and either a title or a patronymic, reminding us of Homer's similar convention, e.g.

456	Hroðgar maðelode,	helm Scyldinga,
529	Beowulf maðelode,	bearn Ecgþeowes:

This formula is always asyndetic, and normally occupies a complete line; it may, however, be varied or amplified by one or more descriptive co-ordinate clauses, as in

925   Hroðgar maðelode,   [he] to healle geong,
        stod on stapole,   geseah steapne hrof. . . .

Other speeches, especially those by minor characters, are introduced more shortly, e.g. by 'word æfter cwæð', 'andswarode', 'spræc ða', 'frægn' or the like; in these there is only one instance of asyndetism, viz.

258   Him se yldesta   andswarode

although, it may be observed, we have the connective in the very similar line

340   Him þa ellenrof   andswarode | wlanc Wedera leod.

If a speech is followed by action and not by another speech, the sentence describing the action is always of the *com ða* form or its equivalent; the one apparent exception is 'dyde him' instead of 'dyde him ða' in

2809   Dyde him of healse   hring gyldenne,

which may perhaps be taken as a parenthesis since it interrupts, and does not close, a speech.

In *Beowulf* the 'scop' is never reported in direct speech, and the question where the bard's own words begin, e.g. in the Finn episode (1063 *sqq.*) does not therefore arise.

107. In the speeches themselves the chief feature of style is, as we should expect, a greater syntactical simplicity. Short sentences are much more the rule, and they are used without the restrictions observed in the narrative parts. This is true at any rate for proper speeches of address, but it must be remembered that in others there are large stretches of narrative; these are subject to the same rules as narrative elsewhere.

Let us now consider some examples of gnomic and similar short sentences in *Beowulf*.

108. *Gnomic sentences.* Every true epic tradition uses these in passing judgement on a situation; with *Beo.* 455 Gæð wyrd swa

hio scel, 2765 mæg gold on grunde...oferhigian, we may compare
Odyssey xvii. 218 'God maketh like to go with like' and xix. 13
'Iron is a magnet that draweth a man'. Such gnomic sentences in
Beowulf usually close and dismiss an incident already described,
as in

701   mihtig God   manna cynnes
             weold wideferhð.
2890   Deað bið sella
             eorla gehwylcum   þonne edwitlif.

This use needs no comment.

109. There is, however, another use in which the general
proposition enunciated by the gnomic sentence forms a bridge
connecting two particulars, e.g.

476   is min fletwerod,
             wigheap gewanod;...God eaþe mæg
             þone dolsceaðan   dæda getwæfan:
             ful oft gebeotedon   beore druncne...
             þæt hie in beorsele   bidan woldon
             Grendles guðe...

Here 'dolsceaðan' is usually taken to refer to Grendel ('mad or
desperate foe'); *dol-*, however, means 'rash, foolhardy', and this
is not an appropriate epithet for Grendel. The gnomic saying in
which it occurs ('God can easily defeat a rash assailant') has a
point if we regard it as linking the idea of the *retainers'* death
(gewanod) with that of their boasting (gebeotedan); for the
passage continues

             Ðonne wæs þeos medoheal   on morgentid,
             eal bencþelu,   blode bestymed.

The singular 'þone dolsceaðan' is generic (=any rash assailant).

929   Fela ic laþes gebad,
             grynna æt Grendle;   a mæg God wyrcan
             wunder æfter wundre,   wuldres hyrde:
             ðæt wæs ungeara   þæt ic ænigra me
             weana ne wende...bote gebidan

Again the gnome serves to connect the idea of evil endured in the sentence preceding it with that of deliverance (bote) in the sentence following it; and the passage continues quite naturally

Nu scealc hafað
þurh Drihtnes miht   dæd gefremede
ðe wé ealle   ær ne meahton...

referring to Beowulf's prowess in the fight with Grendel.

3060

Weard ær ofsloh
feara sumne;...wundur hwar þonne
eorl ellenrof   ende gefere
lifgesceafta,   þonne leng ne mæg
mon mid his magum   meduseld buan:
swa wæs Biowulfe...
swa hit oð domes dæg   diope benemdon...

We might have expected the first sentence 'the dragon had already slain many a one' to be immediately followed by 'and now Beowulf perished through a curse that he knew not of', but the poet makes the transition by the general reflection ''tis strange in what circumstances a hero shall die when his day comes'; for 'feara sumne' see 171.

In the three following sections we shall deal with some problems relating to figures of speech.

110. *Litotes.* The expression of an affirmative by the negation of its opposite, often with a strong sense of under-statement, is a recognised feature of style in *Beowulf*, e.g.

841

no his lifgedal
sarlic þuhte   secga ænegum

'His death seemed no matter of sorrow to any man',

2363   Nealles Hetware   hremge þorfton | feðewiges

'No cause had the H. to boast of their warfaring',

3126   Næs ða on hlytme   hwa þæt hord strude

'Then was there no casting of lots who should rifle the hoard.'
Sometimes the understatement is ironic as in 1018 nalles facenstafas Ðeod-Scyldingas ðenden fremedon 'treachery, so far, the Scildings practised not', 1575 næs seo ecg fracod hilderince

'the hero still had a use for the blade'. In one or two examples the precise meaning is not at first sight evident, e.g.

```
1071        ne huru Hildeburh        herian þorfte
            Eotena treowe
```

'nor, I trow, had H. cause to praise the loyalty of the Jutes'; it is not clear whether the negative covers the noun 'treowe' as well as the verb, i.e. whether the Jutes were disloyal, or whether they were loyal but H. had no cause to praise their loyalty.

```
3074        Næs he goldhwæte        gearwor hæfde
            agendes est        ær gesceawod.
```

I have suggested (*Med. Æv.* VIII. 3) that this sentence is best construed as a litotes: 'in no wise would he rather have looked upon the owner's golden bounty at the first (when the vessel was stolen)', i.e. 'far rather would he never have set eyes on the treasure'; this makes it a variation of the more usual *ne gefeah he* type.

'Not many' is a frequent litotes for 'none at all', e.g. 2738 ne me swor fela | aða on unriht 'nor ever an oath did I swear falsely', 3029 he ne leag fela wyrda ne worda 'nought did he conceal of deeds or words'. Meiosis is properly a positive and not a negative understatement, as in 713 sumne besyrwan 'to entrap more than one', 2156 sume worde het 'bade me more than once' (see also 95).

111. *Parallelism*. A common rhetorical device is sentence-parallelism, by which the idea in one sentence is repeated in different words, sometimes with an added definition, in a second, e.g.

```
506         Eart þu se Beowulf        seðe wið Brecan wunne,
            on sidne sæ        ymb sund flite?
```

'Art thou the Beowulf that strove with Breca [and] vied with him in swimming on the sea?' The second sentence may be a negative paraphrase of the first, e.g.

```
152                    heteniðas wæg...,
            singale sæce,        sibbe ne wolde
            wið manna hwone
```

'Waged bitter enmity, strife unceasing, [and] would no peace with any man.' Occasionally we have three parallel sentences, e.g.

847 Ðær wæs on blode brim weallende,
     atol yða geswing eal gemenged
     haton heolfre, heorodreore weol
     deaðfæge deop

where the parallelism makes Sievers' 'deop' quite certain; *deop*
(=deep water) occurs even in prose, e.g. *ASC* 897. In the last
line *deaðfage* (death-stained) should be read in place of *-fæge*,
which is used only of persons. Sometimes if the negative sentence
stands first, it returns on itself, as in

445   Na þu minne þearft
    hafalan hydan, ac he me habban wile
    dreore fahne gif mec ðeað nimeð...
    ...no [? ne] ðu ymb mines ne þearft
    lices feorme leng sorgian.

A bimembral sentence may be repeated in the form *abab*, e.g.

453 Onsend | beaduscruda betst þæt mine breost wereð,
    hrægla selest þæt is Hrædlan laf...

or chiastically in the form *abba*, e.g.

1679   on æht gehwearf
    æfter deofla hryre Denigea frean
    wundorsmiþa geweorc, [ond] þa þas worold ofgeaf
    gromheort guma...ond his modor eac,
    on geweald gehwearf woroldcyninga
    ðæm selestan,

where the *ða*-clause answers to 'æfter deofla hryre' (the unidiomatic *ond* should be removed): 'the wondrous work came into the
hands of the Danish prince after the fall of the demons: when the
grim-hearted one, and his mother too, gave up this life, [it] passed
into the keeping of the best of Kings...'. There is a similar
chiastic balance in

1247 þæt hie oft wæron an wig gearwe
    ge æt ham ge on herge ge gehwæþer ðara,—
    efne swylce mæla swylce hira mandryhtne
    þearf gesælde; wæs seo þeod tilu.

where the last sentence answers to 'hie oft wæron gearwe' and should be so punctuated: 'that they were ever ready for the fray both at home and in the field,—whensoever need befel their liege lord were those warriors loyal'. We have yet another example of this chiastic order in

2684   wæs sio hond to strong
        seðe meca gehwane   mine gefræge
        swenge ofersohte,   —þonne he to sæcce bær
        wæpen wundrum heard   næs him wihte ðe sel

where the editors' semicolon after 'heard' spoils the sentence: 'too strong was the hand that o'erstrained with its stroke every sword: whenever he bore to the fray a weapon wondrous hard, he was none the better for it'.

112. *Anaphora.* We have seen (34) that in sentences like

771   Ða wæs wundor micel   þæt se winsele
        wiðhæfde heaðodeorum,   þæt he on hrusan ne feol,

the second *ðæt* is not anaphoric but introduces a consecutive clause dependent on the first *ðæt*-clause. What are we to say of

126   Ða wæs on uhtan   mid ærdæge
        Grendles guðcræft   gumum undyrne;
        þa wæs æfter wiste   wop up ahafen

and other pairs of sentences where adverbs (*nu, siððan,* etc.) appear to be headwords? In all examples of true anaphora in a principal sentence there is a sense of climax; it is felt in St Paul's words II Cor. vi. 2 'Now is the accepted time, now is the day of salvation', and was, no doubt, as evident in Ælfric's version of that passage as in King James's. This sense of climax is entirely lacking in the *Beowulf* passages just mentioned, and there can be no doubt that the right construction in these (see 16) is correlation and that one of the sentences, usually the first, is subordinate to the other. Again in sequences like

963   Ic hine hrædlice   heardan clammum
        on wælbedde   wriþan þohte...;
        ic hine ne mihte,   þa Metod nolde,

where the repetition of the subject-pronoun is in any case un-idiomatic, a climax is out of place; the relation between the two sentences is not climactic but adversative and should be expressed by *ac* instead of the second *ic*. There is, however, no reason for rejecting 'gehwylc' in

> 984   feondes fingras: foran æghwylc wæs,
>   stiðnægla gehwylc,   style gelicost,

where both pronouns are necessary to the apposition; 'each one (i.e. finger) at its tip, every strong claw, was most like steel'.

113. Sometimes it is a noun or adjective that recurs inside the sentence, e.g. 2284 Ða wæs hord rasod, | onboren beaga hord; can this repetition be rhetorical as in Milton's 'Lycidas is dead, dead ere his prime'? It will at once occur to the reader that the appropriate rhetorical device in *Beowulf* is not repetition, but variation, of the selected word, as in

> 1308   syððan he aldorþegn   unlyfigendne,
>   ðone deorestan   *deadne* wisse,

and it is difficult to see what 2284 would gain in rhetorical force by the second 'hord' (see 168). The repetition in

> 1083   ne mihte | wig Hengeste   wiht gefeohtan
>   ne þa wealafe   wige forðringan

'could not fight out (?) the war with H. nor by war wrest from him the sorry remnant' might indeed have a point if the sentence did not already begin with 'Wig ealle fornam'. One at least of the repeated words, perhaps both, must be an echo of the first.

We conclude that anaphora was not a real figure of speech in *Beowulf*.

114. *Some Interpretations.* It was a saying of the great Lachmann that 'the prime requisite of a good interpretation, as of a good emendation, is that it should spring from the thought'; that is to say, an interpretation may be linguistically sound and yet fail through a misunderstanding of what was in the poet's mind. Let us consider a few passages in *Beowulf* where a single word or phrase, wrongly understood, disorders the sense of the whole:

> 1495   Ða wæs hwil dæges
>   ær he þone grundwong   ongytan mehte;
>   sona þæt onfunde   seðe floda begong
>   heorogifre beheold...þæt þær gumena sum
>   ælwihta eard   ufan cunnode.

'Hwil dæges' is usually rendered 'the space of a day' or, more cautiously, 'a considerable part of a day'. Either sense would require a complete recasting of our ideas about the hero; Beowulf is not, like some of the characters in the Irish romances, a more than human person endowed with magical powers (which would be necessary even for an hour-long dive) but a màn, differing from other men only in his extraordinary strength. 'Hwil dæges' here means 'daytime' as in 2320 hord eft gesceat ær dæges hwile, and the sense of our passage is 'It was now daylight before he could gain the bottom, and so the warder of the flood at once discovered his presence there.' The time agrees with what we are told in 1311, where Beowulf is fetched from his bed at first daybreak (samod ærdæge); it would, therefore, be 'already broad day' when he arrived at the mere.

115.

1635

                 hafelan bæron
earfoðlice   heora æghwæðrum
felamodigra;   feower scoldon
on þæm wælstenge   weorcum geferian
to þæm goldsele   Grendles heafod

According to three of the editions *æghwæðrum* here = *æghwylcum*; if so, it should certainly have been emended as a scribal error, for in all the other places (more than forty) in which either of the pair *-hwylc*, *-hwæðer* occurs the poet uses it with precision. There is, however, no need to emend, for the text means what it says. The head was to be carried, as we are told, on a pole, for which two bearers, one at either end, would usually be sufficient, but the task was too heavy for 'either of two' (= any pair), stout men though they were, and therefore four bearers, two at each end, had to be used; and even four found it difficult work.

116.

1944

Huru þæt onhohsnode   Hemminges mæg:
ealodrincende   oðer sædan
þæt hio leodbealewa   læs gefremede,
inwitniða,   syððan ærest wearð
gyfen goldhroden   geongum cempan

If the glossaries are right about the meaning of 'onhohsnian' (put a stop to), one is at a loss to understand why all the editions specially caution their readers against rendering *oðer sædan* 'they told a different tale'; not only is this the natural sense of the expression but the one which the context seems to demand. *Ðæt* in 1944 refers to '*þæt heo feores onsæce æfter ligetorne leofne mannan*' in the lines before ('that she should take a man's life on a lying charge of wrong') and our passage means: 'Hemming's kinsman put a stop to all that, [and] men at their ale had a different story to tell (i.e. that she had mended her ways) so soon as she was given as a bride to the young warrior'.

117.

2156   sume worde het
          þæt ic his ærest ðe   est gesægde,
          cwæð þæt hyt hæfde   Hiorogar cyning

The important word here is 'his', and three things are to be noted about it; first, that it is the genitive not of 'he' (=Hroðgar), as usually taken, but of 'hit' (=hīldesceorp) as is clear from the next line 'cwæð þæt *hyt* hæfde'; secondly, that it is an objective genitive, and thirdly that, as a pronoun standing before *ærest* (*SS* 63), it must bear a stress. The meaning of the line is therefore 'he bade me mention to thee the gift of the byrnie first, because Herogar once possessed it'; the displacement of *ðe* from its normal position (þæt ic ðe hís ærest, *SS* 66) is inexplicable except as a scribal error.

118. Let us now consider a few passages in which a right relation of sentences to each other is essential to a true interpretation of the thought:

1146   Swylce ferhðfrecan   Fin eft begeat
         sweordbealo slíðen   æt his selfes ham,
         siððan grimne gripe   Guðlaf ond Oslaf
         æfter sæsiðe   sorge mændon,
         ætwiton weana dæl;   ne meahte (? -on) wæfre mod
         forhabban in hreðre.   Ða wæs heal roden
         feonda feorum,   swilce Fin slægen,
         cyning on corþre,   ond seo cwen numen,
         sceotend Scyldinga   to scypon feredon
         eal ingesteald...

The interpretation of this passage depends on its relation to the lines before, which describe Hengest's vengeance on the Jutes. The attack on Finn would seem to be carefully distinguished both in time and place from that on his allies, for what else can be the significance of 'eft' and 'æt his selfes ham'? And the characters are different; Guthlaf and Oslaf are mentioned for the first time, while Hengest and his men (Hengestes heap) drop out of the story. The two brothers returned home by sea (1149) to tell their tale there and in the spring evidently came to Finnsburg to take their vengeance; Finn was slain, his hall burnt (?) and his queen taken. 'Ða wæs heal roden...' seems to be the usual transition-clause subordinate to 'sceotend S. to scypon feredon', and the only difficulty is its exact meaning; this is said to be 'when the hall was reddened with enemies' blood'. Elsewhere, e.g. in *Gen.* 2065 ond feonda feorh feollon þicce, *feorh* means 'bodies' but it is surely straining the sense to extend it to 'blood'; and why 'enemies' blood' rather than 'its defenders' blood'?

119.

1945

oðer sædan
þæt hio leodbealewa   læs gefremede,
inwitniða,   syððan ærest wearð
gyfen goldhroden   geongum cempan,
æðelum diore,   syððan hio Offan flet
ofer fealone flod   be fæder lare
siðe gesohte;   ðær hio syððan well
in gumstole,   gode mære,
lifgesceafta   lifigende breac,
hiold heahlufan   wið hæleþa brego

The problem here is the relation of the first and second *siððan*-clauses to each other; both sense and syntax point to their being parallel clauses, the first one subordinate to 'gefremede' and the second to 'breac'. The arrangement of the four sentences is, therefore, chiastic, of the form *abba* (111); and the meaning is 'she wrought no more evil so soon as she was wedded to the young warrior: when once at her father's behest she had come oversea to Offa's hall, she thenceforth had joy there, on the throne, of all that life brought her, famed for her goodness and cherishing high love for the prince of men'. In the text as above punctuated it looks as if the two *siðð̄an*-clauses were meant to be co-ordinate, but the repeated conjunction is then unidiomatic; moreover, we should certainly expect the second 'siððan' to be correlative to the adverb 'siððan' in 1951. The two principal sentences, one negative 'she was no longer the perilous lover' and the other positive 'she settled down to happy married life', are themselves good examples of parallelism; it must be admitted that the order *ðær hio* instead of *hio ðær* in 1951 is exceptional, and perhaps *ðær* stands for a repeated *ðæt* in the long involved sentence; cf. 2871, where *ðæt* is similarly repeated after *secgan*.

120.

2499   þenden þis sweord þolað
           þæt mec ær ond sið   oft gelæste
           syððan ic for dugeðum   Dæghrefne wearð
           to handbonan,   Huga cempan:
           nalles he ða frætwe   Frescyninge,
           breostweorðunge,   bringan moste...

The train of thought here depends partly on the meaning of 'frætwe' and partly on the relation of the *nalles*-sentence to the preceding one. 'Frætwe' is one of those words which take their meaning (treasure, ornament, armour, sword) from the context. Here it should refer to 'sweord' in the sentence before, just as in 2954 frætwum hremig it refers to 'mece' in the sentence before. Let us see if this makes sense. When we have read as far as 'cempan', we assume either that D. was slain at the hand of Beowulf by the sword, thus becoming its first victim, or that the sword was D.'s own and that Beowulf took it as spoil after slaying him. The first assumption is contradicted by 'ne wæs ecg bona' just below, and the second by the *nalles*-sentence which tells us by implication that the sword was one which D. had intended to present to his lord, the Frisian King, just as (2614) Wigstan presented Eanmund's sword to Onela. We infer, therefore, ·that the sword was one which D. himself had taken from some slain enemy and which Beowulf in turn took from D. The gradual and indirect way in which this simple piece of information is unfolded is quite characteristic of the poet's method. 'Frætwe' is usually taken to refer to the necklet which Beowulf received from Hrothgar (1195) and afterwards gave to Hygd; it is, however, a mere assumption that the man whom D. slew was Higelac, and in any case a reference to the necklet here makes the *nalles*-clause irrelevant and meaningless, for Beowulf is explaining how the *sword* first came into his possession. Moreover, it is a long time since the necklet was mentioned.

121.

3038
Ær hi ðær gesegan   syllicran wiht,
wyrm on wonge,   wiðerræhtes ðær
laðne licgean;   wæs se legdraca
grimlic gryrefah   gledum beswæled;

The usual interpretation is: 'But even before that they had seen a stranger being, the loathly worm lying there on the mead opposite.' This seems to me a conceit quite foreign to the poet's mind and art; when he wishes to tell us that one of two events happened first, he describes them in their right order. What then is the alternative? If we make the *ær*-sentence subordinate to the one following, we have the sense which the context demands (we have just been told that they had found B. dead on the sand): 'before they caught sight of the stranger creature...lying there opposite, the fire-drake, grim, dreadfully mottled, was already utterly (*be*-) scorched with flame'. Let us see how the passage continues:

se wæs fiftiges   fotgemearces
lang on legere;   lyftwynne heold
nihtes hwilum,   nyðer eft gewat
dennes niosian;   wæs ða deaðe fæst,
hæfde eorðscrafa   ende genyttod.

Here 'se' is the so-called compound relative (=he who) and by the subject-rule (53) the second and third clauses, being without subject, must be co-ordinate to the first; the whole passage thus makes a single period meaning 'He that measured fifty foot lengths as he lay, he that had been wont to take his pleasure in the air during the night-hours and to come down again to visit his den, was now fast in death, having enjoyed his earth-caves for the last time.' This is the sentence-structure which syntax indicates, and it makes good sense. The whole passage needs repunctuating; see further 187 end.

CHAPTER IX

STRESS IN OLD ENGLISH

122. One cannot read *Beowulf* intelligently without a knowledge of the way in which the OE language was stressed. How can we gain such a knowledge? Since the alliterative measure in which the poem is written was based on the ordinary stress of the spoken language, it may be thought that we have a sure guide in the metre itself. This, however, is not true without large qualifications, for the metrical types vary greatly and it is always possible that we are not using the right type as our criterion for a given group of words; if, for example, the stress on the pronoun is in question in the sentence 'þæt wæs feohleas gefeoht', it is little use going to the metrical type for an answer when some classify it as B (with *þæt* unstressed) and others as Dy (with *þæt* stressed). Let us, therefore, try another method and, beginning with the stress, assume that it was subject to the same rules as in Modern English and see whether the assumption works, i.e. whether when *consistently* applied it always gives us one or another of the accepted metrical types.

It is the rule in Modern English

(i) that nouns, adjectives, verbs (other than auxiliaries), adverbs (except some adverbs of degree) and demonstrative pronouns are stress-words;

(ii) that personal pronouns, relatives, prepositions and conjunctions are normally unstressed;

(iii) that some words normally without stress may acquire rhetorical or position stress.

We have now to apply these rules to the Old English of *Beowulf* and see whether they work.

123. Since nouns, when present, carry the alliteration and therefore necessarily bear stress, we can leave them out of account and begin with adjectives, taking *eal, fela, oðer, swylc* as examples; assuming that these were always stressed, we get the following varieties of metrical type[1] for verses in which they occur:

1222	ealne wideferhð		Dy
1955	ealles moncynnes		Dx
929		Fela ic laþes gebad	E
2426	Fela ic on giogoðe		A
1300	ac wæs oðer in		B
1351		oðer earmsceapen	Dx
178		Swylc wæs þeaw hyra	Dx
2541		ne bið swylc earges sið	+D₂

Let us now deal with verbs in the same way, taking as our examples *het, gebad, hwearf, secean*:

1807	Heht ða se hearda		A
198		het him yðlidan	Dx
1035	Heht ða eorla hleo		Dy
2258		sio æt hilde gebad	B
264	gebad wintra worn		+D₂
356	Hwearf ða hrædlice		Dx
1210	Gehwearf ða in Francna fæðm		+Dy
756	secan deofla gedræg		Dy
2495		secean þurfe	A

and so with the adverbs *a, her, hraðe, oft*:

779	þæt hit a mid gemete		B
930		a mæg God wyrcan	Dx
244	no her cuðlicor		+D
1228	Her is æghwylc eorl		Dy
1310	Hraðe wæs to bure		A
1294	hraðe heo æþelinga		Dx
4	Oft Scyld Scefing		D
2018		oft hio beahwriðan	Dx
444		swa he oft dyde	C

In all these examples, it will be observed, the stress works satisfactorily for every metrical type without exception.

[1] For the metrical types see Sievers' article in Paul's *Beiträge*, vol. X. The *plus* sign before the capital letter indicates anacrusis. Varieties of D type should be noted: Simple D, /|/ / ×; D₂, /| / × /; Dx, / × | /\ ×; Dy (only in *a* verses), / × / × /.

124. There are a number of words which may belong to either of the first two classes according to their grammatical function, e.g. *ǽr, nu, swa, þǽr*, which may be adverbs with stress, or conjunctions without stress; similarly such words as *swylc* and *þæt* may be either demonstratives with stress, or relatives without stress. The difference is easily seen when a *pair* of such words is used in correlation in the same sentence, e.g.

1370		ǽr he feorh seleð,	Dx
	aldor on ofre,	ær he in wille	C
251		Nu ic eower sceal	B
	frumcyn witan...nú ge feorbuend,		Dx
	mereliðende,	minne gehyrað	
	anfealdne geþoht		
3066	Swá wæs Biowulfe,	þa he biorges weard	Dx
	sohte searoniðas...		
	swa hit oð domes dæg	diope benemdon	B
2075	ðær we gesunde	sæl weardodon,	+A
	ðǽr wæs Hondscio	hild onsæge	Dx
1328		Swýlc sceolde eorl wesan,	Dx
	æþeling ærgod,	swylc Æschere wæs	+E
1455	Næs þǽt þonne mætost	·mægenfultuma	+A
	þæt him on ðearfe lah	ðyle Hroðgares	B

Here again both the stressed and the unstressed forms, without exception, give us correct metrical types.

125. By this time the reader will perhaps have become aware that, whereas our classification of the simple A, B and C types agrees throughout with that of Sievers in *Beitr.* x, our classification of the heavier D and E types differs entirely from his; this is because in all the D and E types we have cited he disallows the stress on adjective, adverb or verb which he admits in the simple A, B and C types, so that he makes, e.g. 1807 Heht ða se hearda an A type, stressing the verb, but 198 het him yðlidan a C type, unstressing the verb, and so throughout the whole list in 123, 124. In his later writings, though he made certain modifications which will be mentioned presently, Sievers never changed this classification.

126. Let us now carry our investigation a step further and consider the problem of stress on demonstrative adverbs and

pronouns more particularly. In the sentence-form *þa wæs* the stress on the adverb is certified by many A type verses like

53 *a*   Ða wæs on burgum   Beowulf Scyldinga

since without it no scansion is possible; and the stress works satisfactorily in the heavier metrical types, e.g.

64   Ða wæs Hroðgare   heresped gyfen   Dx
642   Ða wæs eft swa ær   inne on healle... Dy

Sievers allows the stress in the simple A types, but disallows it in the last two examples (as in many others) which he classifies as C and B respectively. The stress on *þær* and *þæt* is similarly certified by A type verses like

847   Ðær wæs on blode   brim weallende
2999   Ðæt ys sio fæhðo...

and this stress again works satisfactorily in the heavier metrical types, e.g.

835   þær wæs eal geador   Dx
       Grendles grape
170   Ðæt wæs wræc micel   Dx
2441   Ðæt wæs feohleas gefeoht   Dy

but in these last three Sievers again disallows the stress, classifying them as C, C and B respectively, and there are many others of the type which are thus treated. *Næs þa (þær, þæt)* is the normal negative form of *þa (þær, þæt) wæs*, and there is no reason to doubt that the adverb or pronoun in this form retained its stress and that the substantive verb was as usual without stress; this suits every place in which the words occur without exception, e.g.

3126   Næs þa on hlytme   hwa þæt hord strude   + A
2591   Næs ða long to ðon   + D$_2$
2555   næs ðær mara fyrst   + D$_2$
1455   Næs þæt þonne mætost   mægenfultuma   + A
2415   næs ðæt yðe ceap   + D$_2$

Sievers' classification of all these is different; in the first and fourth he stresses the verb and unstresses the adverb or pronoun, while in the other three he unstresses both, making the metrical type in each B instead of D.

127. In every language there are some words in which the stress may vary with their position in the sentence, and the reader may ask why the rule for *næs ða* should not be different from the rule for *ða wæs*. The answer is that, whatever be the rule for *næs ða*, that rule must be consistently applied, and it is not consistently applied when the verb is stressed in 'næs ða on hlytme' and unstressed in 'næs ða long to ðon' as Sievers' classifications require. Nor can the analogy of enclitic *ða* in *Cóm ða* be pleaded for the unstressing of the adverb in 3126, for *com* is a stressed verb while *næs*, except in certain positions, e.g. at the end of a line, is unstressed.

128. Let us now go on to examine some other *ða*-combinations. How are we to stress *he ða*? The analogy of Modern English (in 'he thén departed') suggests that the adverb is stressed and that the pronoun is proclitic to it and unstressed; and this gives us good scansion in every place in which the words occur, e.g.

2788	He ða mid þam maðmum	mærne þioden	+ A
1263		he ða fag gewat	+ D₂
3137	Him ða gegiredan	Geata leode	+ A

Sievers makes the first and third of these simple A types, stressing the pronoun and unstressing the adverb; but in 1263 he unstresses both and scans the verse as a simple B type. What of *he ðæt*? We should expect it to follow the analogy of *he ða*, and we find in fact that a stress on the demonstrative pronoun gives us good scansion in every one of the twenty-five places where the words occur, e.g.

798	hie ðæt ne wiston		+ A
632	Ic ðæt hogode		C
2005		ic ðæt eal gewræc	+ D₂
2335		him ðæs guðcyning,	+ D
	Wedera þioden,	wræce leornode.	

Here, again, Sievers makes the first two examples simple A types (stressing 'hie', 'ic') and the other two B and C respectively, stressing neither the personal nor the demonstrative pronoun. If he were consistent he would have 3-lift verses in the many exx. like 2005.

129. There are many more of the *ða*-combinations of which we will mention only three. The first is the adverbial phrase *ða git*. Anyone on first meeting it may well be puzzled where to place the stress; the only way to find out is by trial and error, and we soon discover that the one stress which suits every context is *ða gít*, e.g.

47 *a*	Ða gyt hie him asetton	segen gyldenne	+ A
536		wæron begen ða git	B
1050	Ða gyt æghwylcum...		+ D

Sievers' classification of these is (i) simple A, (ii) B, (iii) C; that is to say, he stresses *ða* in the first, *git* in the second, and neither *ða* nor *git* in the third. A second combination is *ða com*, i.e. one in which *ða* is followed by a stressed verb (see **11**); though in all such sentence-forms Sievers takes the *ða* as a demonstrative adverb, he has the following different scansions:

710	Ðá com of more
2980	ða gebéah cyning
1600	Da com non dæges

that is, he stresses the adverb in the first, the verb in the second, and neither adverb nor verb in the third; his classification of these three verses is A, C, C. Yet a third combination is the supposed double demonstrative in 331 ða ðær wlonc hæleð, 809 Ða ðæt onfunde, 1280 ða ðær sona wearð; the reader will find by trial that the one stress which works everywhere is *ðă ðǽr, ðă ðǽt*, showing that *ða* is the conjunction. The only stress which Sievers admits in the three verses is on *ða* in 809.

130. Having now dealt with examples of all the parts of speech which are normally stressed, we come to those others, viz. personal pronouns and prepositions, which are normally unstressed, but which, under certain conditions, may become stressed. Personal pronouns and possessives acquire a stress, usually called rhetorical stress, if the meaning intended gives them a special emphasis, e.g.

431	þæt íc mote ana...Heorot fælsian		+ A
2657		þæt hé ana scyle	+ E
	Geata duguðe	gnorn þrowian	
2077		hé fyrmest læg	E

2156	sume worde het	
	þæt ic hís ærest ðe est gesægde	C
506	Eart þú se Beowulf se ðe wið Brecan wunne	+A
557	heaðoræs fornam	
	mihtig meredeor þurh míne hand;	B

In four of these examples 'ana' 'fyrmest' 'ærest' (see *SS* 63) are stress-pointing words, in the last the stressed 'mine' alliterates; for 2156 see 117. In the following the stress marks an implied contrast to a noun or other pronoun in the context:

532	Soð ic talige	
	þæt íc merestrengo maran ahte	+D
939	Nu scealc hafað...dæd gefremede	
	ðe wé ealle ær ne meahton	C
	snyttrum besyrwan	
960	Uþe ic swiðor	
	þæt ðú hine selfne geseon moste	+A

In each of these the pronoun is the subject of a subordinate clause; it can, however, equally well be the subject of a principal sentence and, since stress gives to a pronoun the freedom of a noun, it may, as the headword, be separated from its verb, as in

318	Íc to sæ wille	Dx
1412	hé feara sum beforan gengde	D₂
2620	Hé frætwe geheold fela missera	D₂

where the stress marks the contrast to 'eowic', 'æþelinga bearn' and 'his byre' in the adjoining lines.

Sievers never recognises rhetorical stress except in lines like 557 above, where the stressed word happens to alliterate.

131. In the examples so far given the rhetorical stress on the pronoun has not affected its position in the sentence. A different kind of stress is the poetic artifice of *position*-stress, which depends on the fact that any unusual position of a word draws particular attention to it and so tends to give it emphasis. It operates differently with different parts of speech; its effect on a pronoun in any oblique case is to give it *front-position*. In 'fyren hine onwod' the pronoun, standing in its normal position next to the verb, is without stress; but the poet writes (915) 'hine fyren onwod' and the pronoun now has position-stress, as it has in Milton's 'Him the Ammonite | worshipped in Rabba'. Other examples are

258	Hím se yldesta	andswarode	Dx
477		híe wyrd forsweop	D₂
2175		hýre syððan wæs	E
	æfter beahðege	breost geweorðod	
1841	Ðé þa wordcwydas	wittig Drihten	Dx
	on sefan sende		
1853		Mé þin modsefa	Dx
	licað leng swa sel		

The subject in all these is a noun; if a pronoun, it stands before the stressed pronoun and is proclitic to it, as in 426 ic þé nu ða | biddan wille, where the alliteration certifies the stress. Naturally, the stress-rule does not apply to sentences like 'him wæs geomor sefa' where the pronoun has its normal position before the verb. Sievers does not recognise the stress on pronouns with front-position except in the rare case where the pronoun alliterates, as in 426 above.

132. Prepositions and possessive and demonstrative adjectives acquire stress by postposition, e.g.

19		Scedelandum ín	E
41	maðma mænigo	þa him míd scoldon	C
1236	ond him Hroðgar gewat	to hofe sínum	C
2959	freoðowong þóne	forð ofereodon	D
3107	ond þonne geferian	frean úserne	D

This inversion is the rule in the conventional formulae 'Beowulf min' 'wine min' and the like; we find it occasionally with the genitives his and hira, as in 178 swylc wæs þeaw hyra.

133. There is yet another kind of position-stress which affects only possessive adjectives, viz. when the possessive, whether preceding or following its noun, is separated from it by other words, e.g.

| 251 | | nu ic eówer sceal | B |
| | frumcyn witan | | |

1180	Ic mínne can	B
	glædne Hroðulf	
1703	Blæd is aræred...	
	ðín ofer þeoda gehwylce	Dy
2742	morðorbealo maga, þonne mín sceaceð	C
	lif of lice.	

There are thus three ways in which possessives may become stressed, viz. the two kinds of position-stress just illustrated and rhetorical stress.

134. A sort of position-stress is the ictus on certain temporal conjunctions, which only occurs when they stand first in a line, e.g.

9	óððæt him æghwylc ymbsittendra
2092	síððan ic on yrre uppriht astod
2038	ðénden hie ðam wæpnum wealdan moston
2634	ðónne we geheton ussum hlaforde

This ictus is almost entirely confined to dissyllabic words like the above, but it is found occasionally on monosyllables also, e.g.

| 1496 | ǽr he ðone grundwong   ongytan mehte |
| 2204 | ðá˙ hyne gesohtan   on sigeðeode | hildfrecan. |

The stress has, of course, no rhetorical significance.

135. There are some words, in Old as in Modern English, so weak that they can never bear stress; they are chiefly mere link-words like the conjunctions *ond*, *ac*, *ne*, *þæt* and the relative particle *ðe*. These, however, Sievers frequently stresses especially at the beginning of a line, e.g.

71	ónd þær on innan eall gedælan
2973	ác he him on heafde helm ær gescer
157	né þær nænig witena wenan þorfte
431	þǽt ic mote ana...Heorot fælsian
1972	þǽt ðær on worðig
1846	gíf ðæt gegangeð
941	ðé we ealle ær ne meahton
632	íc þæt hogode þa ic on holm gestah

In every one of these the second word has either natural or rhetorical stress, and the verses are all A types with anacrusis;

it is the weak anacrustic syllable which Sievers stresses in every line. We have already pointed out that he does the same in many verses in which *wæs* (*næs*) is the headword, as in

1455   Næs þæt þonne mætost
3126   Næs þa on hlytme

where he stresses the verbs and unstresses the demonstratives. There must be something wrong with a metrical classification which uses stress so inconsistently as has been shown in this chapter, and it is high time to investigate what it is.

N.B. The reader should note that examples in Sievers' article in Paul, *loc. cit.* are as a rule not cited textually but only referred to by number of line under the various classificatory headings, where they sometimes need some searching out.

CHAPTER X

POSTPONED ALLITERATION

136. The chief source of the inconsistencies described in the last chapter would appear to be Sievers' theory of postponed alliteration. Alliteration is said to be postponed when it falls on the second instead of the first stress word in a verse, as in

47   Ða gyt hie him asétton   segen gyrdenne

It occurs most frequently in A types, and Sievers would restrict it entirely to these. It is difficult to understand why he encumbered himself with this rule, since, as we shall presently see, examples occur in every metrical type and in some of them they are abundant. The only reasons which he gives are to be found in a passage in his article (*Beitr.* x. 283) of which the following is a summary: 'There are numerous *a* verses in which alliteration falls on the last syllable but one (or the last but two when the syllable is resolved) as in

720*a*   com þa to récede   rinc siðian.

Since all such verses end in the foot / × /, which only appears in types A and C, they must belong either to A or to C; C is excluded because in this type the first of two adjacent stresses is the stronger. They therefore belong to A.' It is, of course, true that in C verses like 'ofer hrónràde' the first stress is the stronger, since in a compound the stress is subject to the accent-law, but it must be obvious that there may be C verses, as there are A verses, in which the second of two *separate* words has the chief stress and therefore carries the alliteration. It will be observed that Sievers does not mention either B types or the heavier D and E types in his explanation.

137. Let us give some examples of postponed alliteration in *a* verses both of the simple B and C types and of the heavier D types:

459	Gesloh þin fæder	fæhðe mæste	B
391	Eow het sécgan	sigedrihten min	C

4	Oft Scýld Scefing	sceaþena þreatum	D
20	Swa sceal géong guma	gode gewyrcean	Dx
264	Gebad wíntrà worn	ær he on weg hwurfe	+D₂
504	æfre mǽrða þon ma	middangeardes	Dy

What does Sievers do with all these? In answering this question, it will be convenient to confine our attention first to the simple types B and C; the instances are

459	Gesloh þin fǽder	fæhðe mæste	B
779	þæt hit a mid geméte	manna ænig	B
1514	þær him nænig wǽter	wihte ne sceðede	B
3056	he is manna gehýld—	hord openian	B
262	Wæs min fǽder	folcum gecyðed	C
391	Eow het sécgan	sigedrihten min	C
632	Ic þæt hógode	þa ic on holm gestah	C
941	ðe we éalle	ær ne meahton	C
2048	ðone þin fǽder	to gefeohte bær	C
2157	þæt ic his ǽrest ðe	est gesægde	C
2573	ðær he þy fýrste	forman dogore	C

The first three seem flawless examples of a B type with postponed alliterations, the fourth transgresses the Rule of Precedence. Sievers (*Beitr.* 289) hesitates between A and B in classifying the first three, but in his later work, *Altgerm. Metrik* 85, he takes them as 'certainly B'. Kl. in his *Metrical Note* takes 459 and 1514 as possibly B though more probably A, 779 as probably B, and 3056 as certainly B. H. inverts the order in 459, 1514 (e.g. ðin fæder gesloh) so as to remove the postponed alliteration, and emends 3056; in 779, however, he keeps the *a* verse and alters the *b* verse to 'ænig manna', thus destroying the alliteration altogether (since the last stress in a line cannot alliterate) unless indeed he places it on 'a' in the *a* verse contrary to the Rule of Precedence.

138. We pass on to the seven C types in our list. Among these 'het' in 391 and 'þæt' in 632 are stress words by nature; for the rhetorical stress on the pronouns in the other five see 130, and for 2157 in particular 117. Sievers, in *Beitr.* 284 *sqq.*, classifies them all as A types with the exception of 2157 which he makes B; some of the verses, however, he considers short. In *AGM* 85. 5 he suggests the possibility of stress (and alliteration) on a short

syllable instead of a long in certain A types, e.g. on the first syllable of 'lufan' in

1728   Hwilum he on lufan   læteð hworfan,

and similarly in lines like 262 on the first syllable of 'fæder'; such a line, with the false stress which he gives to 'wæs', would then become a normal subtype of A. He does not reject, however, the possibility of 262 being after all a C type with a stress on 'min'. There is certainly one formidable objection to his notion of making a short stress do the work of a long, viz. that there are very numerous instances of *a* verses like 278 þurh rumne sefan, 294 wið feonda gehwone, which in that case become metrically ambiguous; they are usually scanned as B types, but it would now appear that they may just as well be A with anacrusis. Is such a gratuitous confusion of types credible? H. treats 262 and 2048 as short verses and emends them, Kl. classifies them as A_3 types, W.-Ch. rightly make 262 a C type with a rhetorical stress on 'min'. The weightiest objection to the classification of these C types as A lies in the fact that it entails in some of them a stress on words like *wæs, þe* and *þæt* (conj.); *wæs* in OE verse was normally the headword in principal sentences where the subject was a noun qualified by the article or a possessive, and in this position it was invariably stressless, as is proved by abundant instances like 133 *b* wæs ðæt gewin to strang, 146 *b* wæs seo hwil micel, 330 wæs se irenðreat.

139. Let us now go on to examine postponed alliteration in the heavier D and E types, still confining ourselves to *a* verses. If the first stress-word is a noun or adjective it necessarily alliterates and this case therefore need not be considered. Where, however, the first stress-word is some other part of speech, postponement is always possible; here are examples of it where verbs, adverbs and demonstratives occupy the first position in the several kinds of D type:

38	ne hyrde ic cymlicor	ceol gegyrwan	+Dx
264	gebad wintra worn	ær he on weg hwurfe	+D_2
2401	gewat ða twelfa sum	torne gebolgen	+Dy
1228	her is æghwylc eorl	oðrum getrywe	Dy
4	Oft Scyld Scefing	sceaþena ðreatum	D

1294	hraðe heo æþelinga	anne hæfde	Dx
642	Đa wæs eft swa ær	inne on healle	Dy
170	Đæt wæs wræc micel	wine Scyldinga	Dx

The reader's attention is drawn to the fact that these *a* verses are all perfect examples of their metrical types and that in the postponed alliteration the Rule of Precedence is everywhere strictly observed. How does Sievers deal with them? In all of them he disallows the stress on the verbs, adverbs and demonstratives which stand first, and thus reduces the metrical types to simple B or C. The only exception he makes is when the first word alliterates (or, more correctly, shares in the alliteration) as in

| 94 | gesette sigehreðig | sunnan ond monan |
| 325 | setton sæmeðe | side scyldas |

where he allows the stress on the verb, scanning the verses as Dx. This, however, is to confuse stress with alliteration and one consequence of this confusion is that there are many pairs of verses essentially similar yet scanning, according to Sievers, differently, e.g.

| 756 | secan deofla gedræg |
| 1450 | secan sundgebland: |

the first of these he makes a B type, with 'secan' unstressed, and the second a Dx type, with 'secan' stressed; and he does the same with

{1035	Het ða eorla hleo
{1114	Het ða Hildeburh
{3166	Forleton eorla gestreon
{1622	Oflet lifdagas

and many other similar pairs.

140. *Eal* is a striking example of what many words suffer in these scansions; it is a stress-word of almost the first rank in alliterative precedence, standing, as a quantitative adjective, only below nouns and adjectives of quality. Sievers gives it the stress to which it is entitled in

2886	eall eðelwyn
906	eallum æþellingum
2297	ealne utanweard

which he rightly classifies as various types of D; but he refuses
the stress whenever *eal* does not alliterate, as in these examples
of the same three types:

486	eal bencþelu
1955	ealles moncynnes
1222	ealne wideferhð

which he classifies, not as D, but as C, C and B respectively.
Could anything be more absurd?

141. *Postponed Alliteration in b verses.* It will be obvious
to the reader that in *b* verses of A, B or C type postponed
alliteration is impossible for the simple reason that the last
stress cannot alliterate; but it requires only a moment's reflection to see that it is possible in any *b* verse of D type when
the first stress falls on a separate word; we have abundant
examples of verbs, adverbs and demonstratives in this position,
e.g.

78	healærna mæst;	scóp him Heort naman
198	æþele ond eacen.	Hét him yðlidan
291	frean Scyldinga.	Gewítað forð beran
254	furður feran.	Nú ge feorbuend
930	grynna æt Grendle;	á mæg God wyrcan
1370	feorran geflymed,	ǽr he feorh seleð
11	gomban gyldan;	þǽt wæs god cyning
835	earm on eaxle	—þǽr wæs eal geador
1306	freonda feorum.	Ðá wæs frod cyning

All these *b* verses are of the same Dx type and the postponed
alliteration is regular in each one of them; Sievers classifies them
all alike as C types, disallowing the first stress in each. It will at
once be apparent that, since the double alliteration common in
a verses (e.g. gesette sigehreðig) does not normally occur in
b verses, Sievers' rule mentioned in **139** does not operate. It is,
therefore, only when a verb or adverb, occupying first place in a
heavier *b* verse, alliterates in its *own* right, that Sievers allows it
stress, as in

| 603 | guðe gebeodan. | Gæð eft seðe mot |

The consequence, however, is just the same, viz. that we have, in *b* verses as in *a* verses, contrasted pairs like

⎰ 123	þritig þegna;	þánon eft gewat
⎱ 224	eoletes æt ende.	Ðanon úp hraðe
⎰ 603	guðe gebeodan.	Gǽð eft seðe mot
⎱ 455	Welandes geweorc.	Gæð a wýrd swa hio scel
⎰ 992	folmum gefrætwod;	féla þæra wæs
⎱ 929	lungre gelimpe.	Fela ic láþes gebad
⎰ 2863	secg sarigferð	séah on unleofe
⎱ 926	stod on stapole,	geseah stéapne hrof

in which the same word is stressed or unstressed by Sievers according as it alliterates or not. Yet the reader will observe that if every first word in these *b* verses is stressed, as it ought to be, the alliteration is governed strictly by the Rule of Precedence.

142. Our examples so far have been selected to show the reader the *kind* of error which has enabled Sievers to reject postponed alliteration in D and E types, viz. the unstressing in certain positions of verbs, adverbs and demonstratives; some figures must now be given to indicate the *scale* on which this unstressing has been carried out. In *a* verses it occurs 130 times and affects the stress of 27 quantitative adjectives or verbs, 57 adverbs and 46 demonstratives; in *b* verses it occurs 133 times and affects the stress of 40 quantitative adjectives or verbs, 40 adverbs and 53 demonstratives. That is to say, Sievers' scansion in these 263 lines is demonstrably inconsistent with his scansions elsewhere. In this reckoning the adverbs in supposed principal sentences like 'ða of wealle geseah' 'nu ic eower sceal frumcyn witan' and the demonstrative pronouns in clauses like 'ðara ðe tirleases trode sceawode' are not included; if they were, the numbers would be considerably increased.

143. The diminution in the *number* of D types is not the only consequence of Sievers' scansions; another, equally injurious, is the qualitative impoverishment of the type. There is an impressive variety in weight among its examples, arising from the kind of words used in them. Every reader will feel the difference between a D type like 1323 Dead is Æschere, with its two noun-words, and

one like 2117 Ða wæs eft hraðe, with its light adverbs, or between a strong E type like Draca morðre swealt and a weak one like He ðæt sona onfand; yet there is a whole scale of values between these two extremes:

(i) 915*b* freondum gefægra;   hine fýren onwod D_2
     1162*b* win of wunderfatum.   Ða cwom Wéalhðeo forð $+D_2$

In each of these two the one noun naturally alliterates;

(ii) 1903*b* yrfelafe.   Gewat him ón naca $+Dx$
     2152*a* Het ða ín beran   eafor heafodsegn. Dx

In these, adverbs of place rightly take precedence over verbs;

(iii) 2985*a* Ðenden réafode   rinc oðerne Dx
     3178*a* Swa begnórnodon   Geata leode. Dx

In these, verbs rightly alliterate over adverbs of time and manner;

(iv) 2532*b* uncer twega.   Nis ðæt éower sið. $+D_2$
     642*a* Ða wæs éft swa ær   inne on.healle Dy
     2175*b* swancor ond sadolbeorht: hyre sýððan wæs D_2

In these, adverbs of time and possessives take the alliteration over demonstratives and personal pronouns, which rank lowest in the scale and hardly ever carry alliteration.

The rich variety among these and similar examples is completely effaced by Sievers' scansions, which turn them all into simple B and C types by denying stress to the first stress-word in every verse.

144. There is, moreover, a lesser metrical ornament, viz. anacrusis, which suffers heavily in the same way. Anacrusis is an introductory unstressed up-beat which may occur in every metrical type which begins with a stressed syllable, e.g.

107   in Caines cynne $+A$
141   gesægd soðlice $+D$
480   ful oft gebeotedon $+Dx$
1616   forbarn brodenmæl $+D_2$

In most *a* verses of A type and in some of D type (e.g. 141 above) Sievers accepts anacrusis; it is, however, far more frequent than he allows even in *a* verses, for it occurs repeatedly both in the D and E types (139) which he reduces to B and C and in all those

A types (135) in which he gives stress to the first word instead of the second. In *b* verses, except for the eight A types in which he *must* admit it, he makes a clean sweep of anacrusis, for there is here no double alliteration, as there is in the *a* verses (e.g. gesægd soðlice), to preserve it.

145. Klaeber (*Metr. Obs.* 24) asserts that anacrusis was 'studiously avoided in D types in a *b* verse'. Why should it be? There is surely no reason in principle why, if the D type is admitted at all in *b* verses, it should not have anacrusis, just as the A type has. And there are, in fact, several instances of it in D type verses which Sievers, even on his own principles, ought to have admitted, e.g.

501	wæs him | Beowulfes sið
1329	swylc | Æschere wæs
1830	ic on | Higelace wat
402	þa | secg wisode

The first three he scans as B, disallowing the secondary stress in all these proper nouns which he admits everywhere else in an oblique case, e.g. 872 sið Beowùlfes; in 402 he obelises 'ða' (see 53 for this). The right reading (97) in 1830 does, however, make the type B.

146. Apart from these four, there are over ninety instances of anacrusis, in *b* verses alone, among the D types which Sievers turns into B or C, e.g.

7	he | þæs frofre gebad	1201	ge|ceas ecne ræd
331	þa | þær wlonc hæleð	1463	næs | þæt forma sið
336	ne | seah ic elþeodige	2252	ic | nah hwa sweord wege
541	no | he wiht from me	2591	næs | ða long to ðon
825	seþe | ær feorran com	3021	For|ðon sceall gar wesan

To these we may add ten examples out of the many D types in *a* verses which he deprives of anacrusis by making them simple C:

38	ne | hyrde ic cymlicor	1043	ond | ða Beowulfe
452	on|send Higelace	2373	no ðy | ær feasceafte
480	Ful | oft gebeotedon	2410	to | ðæs ðe he eorðsele
630	ond | ða gyddode	2569	Ge|wat ða byrnende
1020	For|geaf ða Beowulfe	3013	ond | nu æt siðestan

Whether anacrusis could be polysyllabic is doubtful, especially in *b* verses (see further 161); in most apparent instances there may have been elision or crasis.

147. We may pause here to summarise our argument in this chapter. We have asked ourselves why Sievers disallowed the first stress in hundreds of verses like

1920*a*   Het ða up beran   æðelinga bearn,

which he classifies, not as Dx, but as C; the answer we have given is that his rule restricting postponed alliteration to A types prevented him from recognising it in any other type. Why then, we may now ask, did he allow the stress on the same verb in a Dx type like

2802   Hatað heaðomære   hlæw gewyrcean

where we have a similar postponed alliteration, the dominant 'stave' being 'heaðo'—though 'hatað' shares in the alliteration? The only possible answer seems to be that the double alliteration misled Sievers into supposing that such verses were examples of normal alliteration, as in

2293   hyldo gehealdeð,

where the dominant is a noun preceding the verb.

The inconsistencies of Sievers' stressings are particularly obvious not only in many pairs of verses like that cited above, in one of which there is double alliteration, but also in other pairs, equally numerous, in which the stress is made to depend not on double alliteration, but solely on the metrical type, e.g.

3058   Ða wæs gesyne   ðæt se sið ne ðah
138   Ða wæs eaðfynde   ðe him elles hwær:

here he admits the stress on *ða* in 3058, an A type, but refuses it in 139, a Dx type, because otherwise he must recognise postponed alliteration in this type, contrary to his rule.

148. There are a few lines in our text in which the Rule of Precedence is broken, e.g.

316   Mæl is me to feran;   Fæder alwalda
2717   Gesæt on sesse;   seah on enta geweorc

The metre here is faulty, for 'mæl' in the first line and 'enta' in
the second ought to take the alliteration, but do not. Similarly, in

344   Wille ic asecgan. . .
           mærum þeodne   min ærende,
655   Næfre ic ænegum men   ær alyfde,
1840   Hroðgar maðelode   him on andsware,

no degree of stress on 'min', 'ænegum' or 'him' can entitle those
words to alliterate over the nouns following them, and once
more the metre is faulty. Since the first passage obviously repeats
the message in

270   Habbað we to þæm mæran   micel ærende

it is possible that in 345 also 'micel' for 'min' is the right reading;
in 655 the removal of 'men' would repair the alliteration.

On the other hand, in some conventional formulae like

197   on ðǽm dæge   ðisses lifes
1395   Ðýs dogor þu   geþyld hafa

the Rule of Precedence seems to have been deliberately overridden
and the exceptional alliteration allowed.

149. Some critics take offence at lines like

1728   Hwilum he on lufan   læteð hworfan
1872   ond be healse genam: hruron him tearas

because a verb alliterates over the noun in the *b* verse; this,
however, is quite regular for, since the last stress in a line is, from
the point of view of alliteration, conventionally silent, there is no
alternative to alliteration on the first stress in any 2-stress *b* verse.
Examples of alliterating verbs in such verses are numerous, e.g.
1128 wunode mid Finne, 1137 fundode wrecca, 1327 ðonne hniton
feðan, 1441 Gyrede hine Beowulf. A special instance is

2863   secg sarigferð   seah on unleofe

where the alliteration is regular if, and only if, the prefix *un-* be
read without stress as in 1756 and elsewhere, the metrical type
thus being A.

CHAPTER XI

METRICAL CRITERIA

150. At all times one of the chief instruments in the textual criticism of verse has been a metrical criterion; a simple example of its application is a passage in Shelley's *Revolt of Islam*:

> Our bark hung there, as one line suspended
> Between two heavens,

where metre supports sense in correcting *one* to *on a*. Let us put beside it a similar example of a missing syllable from *Beowulf*. In the short verse 1546 *a* brad brunecg, idiom demands the conjunction *ond* between two adjectives not synonymous; and metre again supports idiom, for the verse now becomes a good A type. The test is often decisive in dealing with homographs; if there is a doubt whether the sentence 2372 *b* ða wæs Hygelac dead, is principal or subordinate, all doubt is resolved when we find that a stressed *ða* would give us the 3-lift metrical type inadmissible in a *b* verse.

A metrical criterion has special cogency wherever a group of sentences have some feature in common. In the fourteen *b* verses in which (see 3) the headword *ða* is followed by conjunctive order, e.g. ða he hean gewat, the stressed adverb is disallowed because it would give us a 3-lift *b* verse in all of them. Again, the ten *b* verses (21–3) in which *ðær* is followed by conjunctive order, e.g. ðær him hel onfeng, are similarly disqualified as principal sentences, since the adverb *ðær* would be stressed, while the unstressed expletive *ðær* is disallowed by the word-order (75).

151. Our next group consists of the *b* verses in which an oblique case of the pronoun *se* stands first or is preceded only by a preposition:

310	reced...on ðæm se rica bad;
588	ðæs ðu in helle scealt
	werhðo dreogan.
1037	eahta mearas; ðara anum stod
	sadol searwum fah.

1349	ellorgæstas.	Ðæra oðer. wæs
	idese onlic,	
2612	suna Ohteres;	ðam æt sæcce wearð
		...Weohstan bana,
2769	segn...;	of ðam leoma stod,
3014	beagas gebohte;	ða sceall brond fretan.

The pronouns, not being antecedents, should by the prose rule be relatives, and metre supports this construction since the verses all scan as B types. Usually the pronouns are taken as demonstratives, though the metrical type is still held to be B. The demonstrative, however, whether antecedent or not, always has stress, and with the stress we get the 3-lift type in every place except two.

152. For the next group we shall make use of Dx. In this type there are good grounds for holding that a monosyllabic thesis was the rule; excluding the special cases discussed in 154–7, we have sixty-six *b* verses of the type (see exx. in 141) and only one of these is an exception to the rule, viz. 1045 het hine wel brucan (it is noteworthy that the parallel in 2812 het hyne brucan wel, is also anomalous metrically, being a 3-lift *b* verse). Let us now consider the following passages:

1054		ðone ðe Grendel ær
	mane acwealde,—	swa he hyra ma wolde
2522	ac ic ðær heaðufyres	hates wene,
	oreðes ond attres;	forðon ic me on hafu
	bord ond byrnan.	
2646		Nu is se dæg cumen
	...;	wutun gongan to

Word-order tolerates *swa*, *forðon* and *nu* in these three passages as either adverbs or conjunctions, though idiom (27) gives preference to *nu* as a conjunction. What can metre tell us on this point? If the words are conjunctions, the verses in which they stand are all regular B types, if adverbs, the verses are all Dx, but with an irregular dissyllabic or trisyllabic thesis. Metre, therefore, decides in favour of conjunctions. Yet sense requires 2252 to be co-ordinate to a principal sentence: '[and] therefore [I] wear shield and byrnie'. The repeated 'ic', however, in the co-ordinate clause is unidiomatic (51), and without it the thesis in this Dx type becomes perfectly regular. We conclude, therefore, that *swa* and *nu* are conjunctions but that *forðon* is an adverb.

153. We deal next with a problem of correlation:

671	Ða he him of dyde	isernbyrnan...
	Gespræc ða se goda	gylpworda sum
1644	Ða com in gân	ealdor ðegna...
	Ða wæs be feaxe	on flet boren | heafod
251		Nu ic eower sceal
	frumcyn witan...Nu ge feorbuend· | gehyrað
424		ond nu wið Grendel sceal...
	ðing gehegan...Ic þe nu ða
	...biddan wille

Are the two *ða*'s or *nu*'s in each passage correlative, or are they both adverbs as printed in the editions? Poetic idiom (16, 112) is against the latter construction, and metre supports idiom, for if the *ða*'s and *nu*'s are adverbs and therefore stressed, 671*a* is an irregular form of Dx with dissyllabic thesis, 1644*a* is an unknown metrical type with four stresses, and 251*b* and 424*b* are the forbidden 3-lift type.

154. In this and the next two sections we shall consider the *ðara ðe* clauses (see 47) in which there is a false concord; it will be convenient to take them under three heads, (i) those which follow a superlative, viz.

1406	þone selestan	sawolleasne
	þara ðe mid Hroðgare	ham eahtode.
1685	ðæm selestan	be sæm tweonum
	ðara ðe on Scedenigge	sceattas dælde.
2129		hreowa tornost
	ðara ðe leodfruman	lange begeate.
2382	þone selestan	sæcyninga
	þara ðe in Swiorice	sinc brytnade.

In this idiom (see 92) the *ðara ðe* construction is out of place since the superlative is the antecedent, as in 'ðone betstan ðe ic bycgan mæge'. Is there any objection to *ðara* as antecedent on metrical grounds? All the *a* verses in which it is found pose as Dx types, but three of them have a trisyllabic, and the fourth a dissyllabic, thesis. Remove the ðara and we not only mend the false concord but also restore both the idiom after a superlative and the metre, the four *a* verses now becoming simple C types.

155. Our second group consists of the verses (ii) in which the ðara is epanaleptic after *ænig* or *gehwylc*, viz.

842	sarlic þuhte	secga ænegum
	þara ðe tirleases	trode sceawode
996	secga gehwylcum	þara ðe on swylc staráð
1050	Ða gyt æghwylcum	eorla drihten
	þara ðe mid Beowulfe	brimlade teah
1460		næfre hit æt hilde ne swac
	manna ængum	þara ðe hit mid mundum bewand
2250		fyra gehwylcne
	leoda minra	þara ðe ðis lif ofgeaf.

Except for the false concord these are quite normal examples of epanalepsis, the demonstrative pronoun catching up the preceding noun as antecedent of *ðe*, as it does in

936	wea widscofen	witena gehwylcum
	ðara ðe ne wendon...	

which shows both the true concord and, if anyone doubts it, the stress on *ðara*. Besides the false concord, the five exx. in this section share with the preceding group the metrical abnormality of a polysyllabic thesis in Dx, and the excision of *ðara* again removes both anomalies; 'ængum' and 'gehwylcum' now become the antecedents of *ðe* and the metrical types are simple B or C. The forms in the text were no doubt introduced by a scribe familiar with the late WS *ælc ðara ðe* construction.

156. There remains (iii) the group

205	Hæfde se goda	Geata leoda
	cempan gecorone	ðara ðe he cenoste
	findan mihte	
1122		Lig ealle forswealg,
	gæsta gifrost,	ðara ðe ðær guð fornam
1625		sælace gefeah,
	mægen byrðenne,	ðara ðe he him mid hæfde

These are all examples of *false* epanalepsis; in the first two *ðara* refers to the wrong nouns, 'leoda' (instead of 'cempan') and 'gæsta', and in the third it lacks a noun of reference altogether and seems to be the unidiomatic neuter plural found in some Alfredian texts, e.g. *Bede* 210. 31 eall ðaðe he slæpende song, where it is a translation of the Latin *ea quae*. All the exx. are metrically irregular and it can hardly be fortuitous that in this group as in the last two the simple excision of *ðara* repairs both syntax and metre.

157. The polysyllabic thesis in Dx is almost entirely confined to the three groups just examined and to two others, in the first of which there is always a gerund present. The gerund in *Beowulf*, when the verb-stem is long, is usually found only in half lines in which there is no other stress-word, e.g.

174*b*	to gefremmanne
257*a*	to gecyðanne

The exceptions are

473	Sorh is me to secganne
1724	Wundor is to secganne
1941	idese to efnanne
2093	To lang ys to reccenne
2562	Sæcce to seceanne

It will be observed that all these have the metrical abnormality above mentioned. It seems likely, therefore, that the form in all of them was originally the uninflected infinitive, as in 316 Mæl is me to fēran, the metrical type being then simple A. It should be noted that there is nothing abnormal metrically in 1805 fuse to farenne, where *faren-* is a resolved long so that the type is still A. Sievers, followed by some editors, restores the infinitive in four out of the five lines cited.

In the second group, numbering six, the verb-form (*ge*)*truwode* always occurs, e.g. 2370 bearne ne truwode; since dissyllabic thesis occurs with no other similar verb (e.g. wisode), Sievers is probably right in correcting to 'treowde' in all of them, thus making the type A.

158. In the next four sections we shall use a metrical criterion to determine the right *form* of certain words.

In Old, as often in Modern, English when a relative clause following a principal sentence plays the part of subject to that sentence, the relative pronoun is normally without antecedent, as in 'secge se wille' 'Say it who will'. The more usual form, however, in our text is *se ðe*, e.g.

90		sægde se ðe cuðe
603		gæð eft se· ðe mot
	to medo modig	
1003		fremme se ðe wille
1387		wyrce se ðe mote
2766		hyde se ðe wylle

Does this stand for *sé ðe* (=he that) or for WS *seðe*? In all the examples *sé ðe* would give us 3-lift or other abnormal metrical types and may, therefore, be put out of consideration. *Seðe* in late OE (*SS* 117. ii) replaced *se* as the normal relative; is there any metrical objection to it? In the A types, 90, 1003, 1387 and 2766, *seðe* increases the number of syllables in the thesis to three, which is extremely rare in *b* verses and was evidently avoided there; since *se* is found frequently in *Beowulf* in the kind of clause we are considering, e.g.

142		heold hine syððan
	fyr ond fæstor	se ðæm feonde ætwand

it was probably the original form everywhere.

159. Ðæs, ðæs ðe. The stresses in the series *forðón* 'therefore', *forðón* 'because', *forðón ðe* 'because (=for the reason that)' derive logically from demonstrative and relative *ðæt*. They are certified by the scansion in

679	forðán ic hine sweorde	swebban nelle	+A
	'therefore will I not quell him with sword'		
418	forðan hie mægenes cræft	minne cuþon	B
	'because they knew the power of my strength'		
503	forðón ðe he ne uþe	þæt ænig oðer man...	+A
	'because he granted not that any other man...'		

Similarly we have the series *ðæs* 'therefore', *ðæs* 'because, as', *ðæs ðe* 'because'. The stress on *ðæs ðe* is certified by

1628	þæs ðe hi hine gesundne	geseon moston
	'because they could look upon him safe and sound'	

and other lines. The form, however, is disallowed by the metre in many places, e.g. 108*b* ðæs ðe he Abel slog; in these it was perhaps the late pleonastic relative without stress, like Ælfric's *ðider ðe*, *ðonan ðe*, and may have been imported by the scribe. The analogical form *ðéah ðe* is certified by lines like

1130   þeah ðe he (ne) mihte   on mere drifan

which do not scan without the stress; but the metre again disallows it in many *b* verses.

Probably both *ðæs ðe* and *ðeah ðe* were used by the poet, but only when metrically appropriate. Sometimes either form gives good scansion in the same sentence, e.g. 383 ðæs ic wen hæbbe (C), 3000 ðæs ðe ic wen hafo (Dx).

160. *Ymb, ymbe.* There are in *Beowulf* nineteen instances of *ymb* as a preposition to four of *ymbe*, and five of *ymb-* in compounds to three of *ymbe-*; the weight of numbers therefore strongly favours *ymb* as preposition. It is noteworthy that all the seven *ymbe*'s are in the part of the MS. written by the second scribe; they may well be due to him and not to the poet. Metre is neutral as regards the prepositions, since all the verses scan equally well with either form, but it is fairly decisive against *ymbe-* in compounds, one of the three instances being *ymbesittenðra* in 2734 (cf. 9 *ymbsittendra*) and another *ymbefeng* in

2691   heals ealne ymbefeng

where the polysyllabic thesis in this metrical type is abnormal; it only seems to be met with elsewhere in the *ungemete* verses, which are suspect on other grounds (see 94). Sievers reads *ymb-* in

2296   hlæw oft ymbehwearf,

but the polysyllabism in 2691 above is at least as offensive.

Ymbe is the regular form of the adverb both in prose and verse.

161. *Polysyllabic Anacrusis.* We may consider here the lines in which the weak form *wile* (=*wille*) occurs; four out of the five are *b* verses, viz.

346   gif he us geunnan wile

446
1181
       arum healdan
1832

ac he me habban wile
ðæt he ða geogoðe wile

ðæt he mec fremman wile

The effect of reading 'wile' instead of 'wille' is to convert all the verses from A types into B types. Why B rather than A? It can only have been to avoid the long anacrusis in an A type which the normal 'wille' would necessitate. The inference is obvious that polysyllabic anacrusis was deliberately excluded; in fact, there are grounds for thinking that in the stricter scansion of the *b* verse monosyllabism was the rule, but that dissyllabism was admitted in *a* verses. We deal, finally, with (1) a problem of stress; (2) an alliteration test.

162. *No ðy ær.* An example like

2466   No ðy ær he ðone heaðorinc   hatian ne meahte

shows that one word in this phrase must bear a stress, and the only stress which suits this and the other five places is *no ðy ǽr*, *no* being proclitic to *ðy ær* which forms one syllable by crasis; e.g. 1502 no ðy ær in gescod (+D₂), 2160 no ðy ær suna sinum (+D). This proclitic *no* is confirmed by other combinations in which it precedes other forms of the demonstrative, e.g. 2354 no ðæt læsest wæs (+D₂), 1366 no ðæs frod leofað (+D).

Sievers stresses the phrase as *nó ðy ær* in 2466, but in the other five places he disallows stress altogether, scanning them as B or C.

163. *Alliteration test.* Examples abound of the 3-lift *a* verse where each of the three stresses falls on a *separate* word; in these there are invariably two alliterating words, e.g. 625 grette Geata leod, 756 secan deofla gedræg. In many of them the first stress-word is a demonstrative, e.g. 642 ða wæs eft swa ær, 980 ða wæs swigra secg, 1063 ðær wæs sang ond sweg, 2441 ðæt wæs feohleas gefeoht; in these the alliteration is always on the second and third words, never on the demonstrative.

Let us now apply the same test to the *a* verses in which (see 3 *sq.*, 21, 37) an initial *ða*, *ðær* or *ðæt* is wrongly taken as a demonstrative and which thus become 3-lift verses. They are sixteen in number, viz.:

32	ðær æt hyðe stod	74	ða ic wide gefrægn
194	ðæt fram ham gefrægn	229	ða of wealle geseah
415	ða me ðæt gelærdon	465	ða ic furðum weold
662	ða him Hroðgar gewat	1365	ðær mæg nihta gehwæm
2095	ðær ic ðeoden min	2137	ðær unc hwile wæs
2369	ðær him Hygd gebead	2484	ða ic on morgne gefrægn
2694	ða ic æt ðearfe gefrægn	2752	ða ic snude gefrægn
2773	ða ic on hlæwe gefrægn	3134	ða wæs wunden gold.

Without exception they fail to answer the test, the double alliteration everywhere being absent. Metre thus supports syntax in disqualifying them all as principal sentences.

The two exceptions to the rule, 1677 ða wæs gylden hilt, 3166 forleton eorla gestreon, become regular if we write Gyldenhilt, eorlgestreon (cf. 2244).

CHAPTER XII

SCRIBAL ERROR AND ITS SOURCES

164. It will be well at the outset to give the reader some idea of the number and kind of scribal errors in the text of *Beowulf*; they differ, naturally, in the different editions, the more so as emendations approved in notes are not always admitted to the text. Let us take, however, as a basis the most recent of the editions, that of Klaeber, which presents a comparatively con-servative text. The corrections actually admitted number over 250. Of these forty-three are in verses where the alliteration fails, and thirty in verses which are short (not counting the fifteen which are also short among the forty-three first mentioned); it will be clear from these figures that the scribe can have had little sense of the metrical structure of the work which he was copying. In sixty places the inflectional syllable of noun, adjective or verb is either omitted or miswritten; in some of these, e.g. 947 secg betsta, 2673 bord wið rond, the verse is short as well. There are thirty-four instances of wrong, and often meaningless, stressed words, e.g. 306 grummon, 457 fyhtum, 1020 brand=bearn, 1275 þeod=deað; and twenty-four instances of small unstressed words (prepositions, pronouns and conjunctions) either omitted or corrupted. Finally, there are over sixty words in which a letter is dropped or inserted or changed; while many of these are obvious slips of the pen, a fair number are misspellings which might destroy or distort the sense, e.g. 447 deore=dreore, 84 secg=ecg, 1529 hord=hond, 2771 wræce=wræte.

165. There are, moreover, in all the editions numerous errors, of a kind usually counted scribal, which are left as they stand in the manuscript, many of them like the false concords in Cap. VI entailing gross breaches of syntactical law. Nothing indeed is so remarkable in the textual criticism of *Beowulf* as the fact that commentators in general ascribe metrical mistakes to the copyist and therefore correct them, while they attribute the far more glaring syntactical anomalies to the poet and therefore let them stand. Why this difference of treatment? The question we ask ourselves is the same in both cases, viz. whether exceptions come from the author and so invalidate the rule, or come from the scribe and are therefore to be corrected by the rule. The way in which we answer this question in a particular case will naturally differ with the degree of cogency in the evidence. Let us consider a few examples.

166. An isolated exception may be dealt with by the rule of simple probability. We have, e.g. a dative government in

2828   ac him irenna   ecga fornamon,

which some editors defend, although the poem has the accusative in all the other eleven places, one of them being the almost identical 'ac hyne ecg fornam(2772)'. Is it then more probable that 'him' in 2828 comes from the poet, or that it comes from the scribe who elsewhere has admittedly miswritten *hine* as *him*? Again, in

991   Ða wæs haten hreþe   Heort innanweard
             folmum gefrætwod

the anacoluthon 'gefrætwod' is defended by two editors as a passive infinitive with *wesan* understood; but the regular idiom after *hatan* is the active infinitive even where the passive would give sense, as can be seen in all the other thirteen places where the infinitive is used, e.g. 198 het him ȳðlidan godne gegyrwan 'ordered a good ship to be prepared for him'. Which, then, is the more probable, that the poet wrote the passive in one place out of fourteen or that the scribe, forgetting 'haten' and with a different kind of sentence in his mind, wrote Ða wæs...Heort innanweard gefrætwod? In

3077   Oft sceal eorl monig   anes willan
             wræc adreogeð

we have a similar mistake; the scribe, or perhaps the poet, forgetting 'sceal', wrote the more usual finite verb, which all editors rightly correct to 'adreogan'. The two cases are on all fours, and the infinitive should be restored in 992.

167. That most necessary instrument of textual criticism, collation, fails us in *Beowulf* because there is only one MS.; yet

we can learn a good deal about the accidents of scribal transmission by examining two small texts, *The Soul's address to the Body* and *Brunanburh*, of each of which more than one transcript happens to have survived. Of *Soul's address*, less than 130 lines long, there are two MSS., *Exeter* and *Vercelli*, of which *E* is usually the better; they differ frequently in the omission or insertion of small words like prepositions (four), pronouns (five), eal (two), her (two), in the inflections of nouns (five) or verbs (six) and in the forms of the relative pronoun (five); alliteration fails five times (four in *V*), and there are four short verses (all in *V*). A few of the greater variations may be illustrated more fully:

33 *E*	ic þe in innan	no ic þe of meahte
33 *V*	Eardode ic ðe on innan	ne meahte ic þe of cuman
51 *E*	se ancenda,	*V* se acenneda
69 *E*	Gode lifgendum	lofsang doð, *V* lifg. Gode
116 *E*	bið seo tunge totogen	
116 *V*	beoð hira tungan totogenne	
122 *E*	he þa tungan totyhð,	*V* þæt he t. t.
129 *E*	modsnoterra,	*V* modsnotra gehwam.

Brunanburh is a poem of seventy-three lines; of the numerous small variations recorded in Plummer's *Chronicle* only two kinds need be mentioned, viz. the omission or insertion of *ond* (three times) and the differences in the form of the relative pronoun (*ðe—þara ðe, þæs—þæs ðe*). The variants in both texts have thus a strong family likeness to those assumed in *Beowulf*, though the omission (or insertion) of small unstressed words is relatively much more frequent in both than it is usually assumed to be in that poem.

168. Collation failing us in *Beowulf*, we may still learn something by classifying the most likely sources of unconscious error on the part of the scribe in places where error is generally admitted.

(i) *Echo*, causing the mechanical repetition of a sound; it may affect (*a*) single letters or syllables; (*b*) whole words. Of (*a*) there are abundant examples, e.g. 1830 on Higelace wac (=wat), 1991 wiðcuðne (=wid-), 1362 stanðeð (=standeð), 2706 gefyldan (=-e), 2829 hearde heaðoscearde (=-scearpe), probably 1005 nyde genydde (cf. 2680 niðe genyded), 2003, 2542 worna fela (both from the second hand); not infrequently the scribe has corrected himself, as in 2671 where 'fyrwyrmum' is altered to 'fyrwylmum'. This literal error is sufficient in itself to account for 'deog' in 850 deaðfæge deog, 'hyt' in 2649 þenden hyt sy, 'ætgifan', a *hapax*, in 2878 ætgifan æt guðe, and therefore to justify Sievers' and Kemble's emendations 'deop' and 'hat' (cf. 2780) in the first two; 'ætgifan' probably stands for 'agifan' in the third.

In (*b*) the error works with a difference, for the affected word is often widely separated from its contaminator, e.g. 1868 het inne (=hine; 'inne' from two lines before), 2505 ac in cempan gecrong (=campe; 'cempan' from three lines before), perhaps 1909 forð ofer yðe (where the last two words may have come from 'ofer yðum' just above). It should be observed that in all such (*b*) instances it is the *second* word which echoes the first, so that in

2283   Ða wæs hord rasod,
         onboren beaga hord,

it is the second 'hord', not the first, which, if either, needs correction (see 113).

169. Some other likely examples of this kind of corruption may be given:

67   magodriht micel.   Him on mod bearn
       þæt (he) healreced   hatan wolde,
       medoærn micel,   men gewyrcean
       þonne yldo bearn   æfre gefrunon.

'micel' in 69 looks like an echo of 'micel' standing in the same position in 67; and since 'men' as object of 'hatan' is also unidiomatic and better unexpressed, Bright's emendation of 69 'medoærn micle mare gewyrcean' is at least probable:

989   ðe ðæs ahlæcan
       blodge beadufolme   onberan wolde.
2493   Næs him ænig þearf
       þæt he...in Swiorice   secean þurfe
       wyrsan wigfrecan.

In the first, Sievers' emendation of 'wolde' to 'mihte' on the ground of sense is supported by its being possibly an echo of 'wolde' at the end of 988; in the second, Bugge's 'þorfte' removes the false tense-sequence but not the tautology, and 'scolde' would be better: 'þurfe' is simply an echo of 'þearf'. Some other possible instances are

1082	ðæt he ne mehte	on þæm meðelstede
	wig Hengeste	wiht gefeohtan
	ne þa wealafe	wige forþringan
2674	geongum garwigan	geoce gefremman,
	ac se maga geonga....	

The repetition of a word in the same sentence (wig wige, geongum geonga) is very unlike the poet; elsewhere 'mæra' goes with 'maga', and it would give us the usual double alliteration here, but 1082 is more complicated since 'wig' occurs again at the beginning of the sentence (see 113). In 1033 'wið Hengeste' is an obvious correction but it changes the alliteration.

170. The most remarkable instance of unconscious reminiscence is

1512	Ða se eorl ongeat
þæt he in niðsele	nathwylcum wæs
þær him nænig wæter	wihte ne sceþede,
...fyrleoht geseah...	
Ongeat þa se goda	grundwyrgenne,
merewif mihtig,	mægenræs forgeaf
hildebille;	

Here the second 'ongeat', whether with the same or a different sense, is surely intolerable; it seems to be a clear case of echo, and the simplest emendation is 'ongean', which yields good sense: 'When the earl perceived that he was in some hostile hall...[and] beheld the light of fire, then against the hag of the abyss he let drive with his battle-bill.' *Ongean* often takes the accusative when it stands before its noun, as in *Jud.* 165 ongean ða ðeodnes mægð...ðrungon and urnon.

171. (ii) *Similarity of appearance.* Of this source of error examples are equally numerous, e.g. 902 earfoð=eafoð, 1333 gefrægnod=gefægnod, 2793 giogoðe=giohðe, 3059 gehydde= gehyðde, mægnes=mæges (more than once), probably 86 ellengæst=ellorgæst, possibly 2035 biwenede=bi werede; the scribe

has himself corrected ellengæst in 1617, and biwerede in 1821. Other probable examples are

2047   meaht du min wine   mece gecnawan,

where the alliteration breaks the rule of precedence; the abnormal order of 'min wine' suggests 'mægwine' as the right word: it restores not only the alliteration but also the sense (clansman), the person addressed being a 'geong cempa'.

953   þu ðe self hafast
              dædum gefremed   ðæt ðin dom lyfað:

the right verb for a *ðæt*-clause is 'gefered' (e.g. 1221 Hafast ðu gefered ðæt ðe...weras ehtigað) and with this emendation there is a gain in simplicity over the accepted 'mid dædum'; 'gefremed' looks like an echo of 940 dæd gefremede.

3061   Weard ær ofsloh
              feara sumne;

the sense of 'feara sumne' given in most notes ('one among a few others') is impossible except where *sum* is in apposition to a noun or pronoun, as in 1412 he feara sum; standing alone *sum* means 'one' or, by meiosis, 'many a one', cf. 713 sumne besyrwan. This contradicts 'feara', which must therefore represent some other word, e.g. 'fara' or 'feora' (='lives'; we have *fea* for *feo* in 156); the statement in 2333 Hæfde ligdraca leoda fæsten gledum forgrunden, surely implies considerable loss of life.

3110   Het ða gebeodan...
              hæle hildedior   hæleða monegum,

Of this it need only be said that, if *hæle* be the same word as *hæleð*, as the glossaries tell us, the poet would hardly have used both in the same line, and 'hæleða' perhaps represents a word similar in form (? 'holdra', qualifying 'boldagendra').

172. Among unstressed words, *ða*, *ðæt* and *ðe* provide frequent examples of error arising from similarity of appearance. The question has been debated whether the symbol þ (=*ðæt*) could also be used for *ða*. This, however, is to pose the problem too narrowly, for it is quite clear that the *three* words *ða*, *ðæt*, *ðe* were frequently confused by the *Beowulf* scribe; we have

(ðæt = ða)	3134	Ðæt wæs wunden gold	on wæn hladen
(ða = ðæt)	2629		ða se wyrm onfand
(ðæt = ðe)	14		fyrenðearfe ongeat,
		ðæt hie ær drugon	aldorlease
(ðe = ðæt)	242	ðe on land Dena	laðra nænig
		mid scipherge	sceððan ne meahte.
(ðe = ða)	1000	hrof ana genæs...ðe se aglæca
		on fleam gewand	

In 3134 three editors read *ða*, one *ðær*; in 2629 all four editors read
ðæt; in 14 two editors read *ðe* which is undoubtedly right in a
limiting relative clause (we have the same words with *ðe* in 831,
1858); in 1000 two editors read *ða*, two *ðe* which, however, cannot
be justified by the analogy of 2400 oð ðone anne dæg ðe he wið
ðam wyrme gewegan sceolde, where *ðe* is relative and there is a noun
antecedent; in 242 *ðe* for *ðæt* in a final clause is a *hapax* unless we
take 'laðra' as a comparative, which is what the scribe may have
done (cf. *ðe læs*). It will be obvious to the reader that the errors
in these passages make it unsafe to appeal to MS. authority in other
cases (and they are not wanting, see **31, 32, 103**) where one of the
group *ða, ðæt, ðe* is under suspicion. There does not seem to be any
certain evidence for the confusion of *ðæt* with *ðær*, though some
editors assume it in 3134.

173. A special case of similarity of form is wrong division of
words, e.g. 924 medostig gemæt (=medostigge mæt), 1454 brond
ne (=brodne) beadomecas, 2305 wolde fela ða (=se laða), possibly
900 he ðæs ær onðah (=aron ðah), 2278 ðreo hund wintra (=ðusend),
3084 heold on (=healdan). In 2385 He þær orfeorme (=He ða
for feorme) the first *f* has been misread as *r* and then added to the
wrong word. If Cosijn's 'healsbege' is the right reading in 1214
Heal swege onfeng, it can hardly stand in this form as it leaves
the verb without a subject; personification is idiomatic in this
kind of sentence, e.g. 688 hleorbolster onfeng eorles andwlitan,
and the right division is therefore 'heals bege onfeng'.

So far the scribal errors have given us wrong words; our next
source accounts for many instances of wrong syntax.

174. (iii) *Syntactical attraction.* In this a word has been altered
through being construed in a false grammatical relation to a

neighbour word. Obvious examples are 1903 gewat him on nacan
(=naca), 2448 ond he him helpan ne mæg (=helpe, object of
'gefremman'), 2769 of ðam leoman (=leoma) stod, probably
282 ond þa cearwylmas colran wurðaþ (=wurðan, after 'sceolde').
In 224 'eoletes' perhaps developed in two stages; first, the last
syllable of *ealad* (see 187) became -*et*, echoing *æt* which follows,
and then *ealet* was made a genitive on the analogy of phrases like
'ealdres æt ende'. The interchange of *ea* and *eo* is an Anglianism.

All or most editors correct the cases to Sigemundes, Weohstan,
Hygelaces, in

875	ðæt he fram Sigemunde	secgan hyrde,
	ellendædum	
2612	ðam æt sæce wearð,	
	wræccan wineleasum,	Weohstanes bana
2957		ða wæs æht boden
	Sweona leodum,	segn Hygelace
	freoðowong ðone	forð ofereodon,

and some also correct

2777	Bill ær gescod
	—ecg wæs iren—	ealdhlafordes
3066	ða he biorges weard
	sohte, searoniðas:

to -hlaforde, searoniða (adv. gen.); the objection to 875 and 3066
is that two nouns like 'Sigemunde' and 'ellendædum', not being
in pari materia (see 81), make a false apposition. In

1709	ne wearð Heremod swa,
	eaforum Ecgwelan,	Ar-Scyldingum

read 'eafora' (=son); both sense and usage favour apposition to
the preceding noun; it may be added that *a* and *ū* were often
confused. It is possible that the anomalous 'gewearð gewrecen'
(95) in

3061	ða sio fæhð gewearð
	gewrecen wraðlice

is an instance of syntactical attraction, the scribe having changed
'gewræc' (co-ordinate to 'ofsloh') into the participle; 'gewearð'
in the ða-clause would thus have its normal sense: 'when the
feud began'.

175. An instance of a different kind is

2836   Huru þæt on lande   lyt manna ðah
              mægenagendra   mine gefræge,
              þeah ðe he dæda gehwæs   dyrstig wære,
              þæt he wið attorsceaðan   oreðe geræsde;

Here the difficulty of taking 'lyt manna' (=few men) either as
subject or indirect object of 'ðah' is generally recognised, but it
does not seem to have been observed that any collective sense of
lyt as a noun is forbidden by the singular pronoun of reference 'he'
in each of the three following clauses; 'lyt' is, therefore, the adverb,
but the scribe, thinking of the more usual noun construction,
wrote a genitive plural after it instead of a dative (? *mannan*).

1221   Hafast þu gefered   þæt ðe feor ond neah
              ealne wideferhð   weras ehtigað

Is not the right form 'ealle' (='that all men for ever shall honour
thee')? 'Ealne' qualifying 'wideferhð' is tautological and a
distinct weakening of the sense. A likely instance of syntactical
assimilation is

3114   Nu sceal gled fretan,
              Weaxan wonna leg,

where the -*an* of 'weaxan' may well have come from 'fretan'.
Reading 'weax-wonna', we have (1) a typical adjective of colour,
cf. wolcnread, wyrmread, etc., (2) a common syntactical pattern
in which an adjective is attached to the appositive noun, e.g.
92 eorðan worhte, wlitebeorhtne wang, 2724 ofer benne spræc,
wunde wælbleate. The sense of *weax-wonna* would be 'dull or
murky yellow', cf. *goldbeorht*='bright yellow'; for the noun-prefix
weax- cf. 'wax-yellow' in English, German and other languages.

176. (iv) *Haplography, Dittography*. If a word or syllable is
immediately repeated, it is not infrequently overlooked by the
scribe and dropped, e.g. 987 egl(u) unheoru, 1037 þara (on) anum
stod sadol; the two words or syllables may be only approximately
like each other, as in 652 (ge)grette ða, 667 (se) sundornytte
beheold, 1513 þæt he (in) niðsele, 1559 þæt (wæs) wæpna cyst,
possibly 3123 under inwithrof (hror) hilderinc. In

2800   fremmað gena | leoda þearfe

we should certainly expect the pronoun to be expressed, but 'ge gena' is better than the suggested 'ge nu', which does not scan.

177. A special case of haplography is *Homoeoteleuton*, where the similarity of two words or syllables at some distance from each other may cause the scribe to jump the interval and omit all the intervening words; a good example, and a certain one, is *Soul's Address* 107 *E*:

> ne mæg him ondsware   ænige secgan
> ne þær edringe   ænge gehatan:

for this *V* has only the single line

> ne mæg him ondsware   ænge gehatan:

the scribe having skipped from one *ænige* to the other and left out everything between. The same kind of error probably accounts for some of the longer lacunae in *Beowulf*, e.g.

389   Deniga leodum.   (Ða wið duru healle
         Wulfgar eode,)   word inne abead:

this is Grein's emendation, but the bracketed words are not a possible principal sentence and, if they are intended as subordinate, 'abead' has then no subject. Something like

>   þa he wið duru æthwearf,
> Wulfgar hæleðum   word inne abead:

may be suggested 'returning towards the door, W. spoke to the warriors from within'; the similarity of -*leðum* to *leodum* is close enough to account for the omission of the intervening words. So also in

403   under Heorotes hrof   (heaðorinc eode)

'herewisa for' is more likely, since the verb is sufficiently like -*rof* to account for the jump. And again in

2792   breosthord þurhbræc   (   )
         gomel on giohðe   gold sceawode;

some word like Schücking's *gespræc* probably stood at the end of the first line.

178. In *dittography* a word is written by the scribe twice over. Instances with small unstressed words are often corrected by the

scribe himself and need no comment. We have a stress-word repeated in

1376   Nu is se ræd gelang
         eft æt þe anum.   Eard git ne const,
         frecne stowe,   ðær ðu findan miht
         fela-sinnigne secg;   sec gif ðu dyrre.

where *secg* is a dittograph of the four following letters, and the result is a verse which is too long; as to 'fela', I have suggested (*Med. Æv.* VIII. 3) that it is a misreading of 'sele' (cf. 2305 fela ða = se laða) and that the meaning of the passage, read as a single period, is 'Since help is again in thee alone [and] thou knowest not yet the abode, the fearsome place, where thou mayst find the hall of the evil ones, seek if thou dare'; the monsters' home is called 'niðsele' in 1513.

179. There can be no doubt that the omission of a stress-word was sometimes due to the fact that the sense appeared to be complete without it, as in

138   þe him elles hwær
         gerumlicor   ræste (   ),

where 'ræste' was probably taken for the verb,

149   forðam (   ) wearð
         ylda bearnum   undyrne cuð,
586   no ic ðæs (   ) gylpe.

In these two, as elsewhere, the omission affects the alliteration (see further 184). This sense of completeness may account also for short verses like 947 secg betsta, 2673 bord wið rond,

2354   No þæt læsest wæs
         hondgemot,

in all which an unstressed inflection is needed to restore the metre.

180. (v) *Metathesis* is another source of error. It may affect (*a*) the order of letters in a word, e.g. 1200 fealh (=fleah), 1278 ðeod (=deað), 2186 Wereda (=Wedera), 3139 behongen (=behengon), or (*b*) the order of words in a sentence, e.g.

2490   Ic him ða maðmas (= Ic ða him; see 13),
932   ðæt ic ænigra me

(=ic me ænigra, the normal order: cf. 1772),

1266   geosceaftgasta,   wæs ðara Grendel sum

(=ðara wæs; the relative is wanted, not the stressed demonstrative, which gives us a 3-lift verse). In

1833   weordum ond worcum

the stem-vowels have been transposed, and in

1902   maðma ðy weorðre
2710   siðast sigehwile (=siðest sigehwila; see 91),

the inflectional vowels. For a possible metathesis of the stems in 2384 him dæt to mearce wearð, see 187.

A fertile source of the transposition of words is the substitution by the scribe of prose for poetic order. In verse the postposition of certain normally unstressed words, e.g. prepositions and possessives (see 132), gives them a stress which may be essential to the scansion, as in

41   þa him mid scoldon
2729   Nu ic suna mínum   syllan wolde
1959   wisdome heold | eðel sínne
2959   freoðowong ðóne   forð ofereodon

where the normal prose order 'mid him scoldon', 'nu ic minum suna', etc. would leave the verses a stress short. Yet this is the order which the scribe has substituted in 923 ond his cwen mid him, 1984 sinne geseldan, 2376 oððe þone cynedom, 2815 mine magas. The *rhetorical* stress which possessives and other words (130) sometimes bear has no meaning here and is not to be thought of; postposition should be restored. In

2615   brunfagne helm,   hringde byrnan,

we have a different kind of anomaly, since here the alliteration breaks the Rule of Precedence; the words in one of the two half lines should be transposed. Some editors, however, needlessly change the order in lines like

459   gesloh ðin fæder   fæhðe mæste,

where the Rule of Precedence is already strictly observed.

181. There is one kind of corruption which our text has escaped, viz. that which is imported by a too clever scribe who thinks that he knows what his author ought to have written and 'mends his book' accordingly. Our two scribes were immune from this weakness; they were conscientious, if unintelligent, copyists who set down what they saw or thought they saw in their book (perhaps itself a copy) without worrying about sense or metre. There is one great advantage in this faithful form of transcription; for, by studying the different kinds of involuntary error to which it is subject, we can usually correct with confidence either nonsense or wrong sense, as in 1214 heal swege onfeng (=heals bege; see 173), 1278 sunu ðeod wrecan (=suna deað), 2961 ecgum sweordum (=sweorda); often the alliteration makes its contribution, as in 2305 wolde fela ða (=se laða), 2921 mere wio ingasmilts (= Merewioingas milts), 2385 he ðær orfeorme (=he ða for feorme).

These examples bring us to the more general problem of correcting error. The first and most important task of an editor is the 'making of a text', that is, the restoration of the form presented by the MS. to that intended by the author. Can any definite rules be formulated for emending the text of *Beowulf* as transmitted to us? It will be convenient to deal with this problem under several heads, beginning with the simplest cases of error.

182. For merely grammatical faults, e.g. a wrong inflection, there is usually no alternative but the correct form, and in that case the emendation, if good in sense and metre, is certain. If the corruption extends beyond the inflection, the old rule holds that, of two or more conjectures, which are good in sense and metre, the one which assumes the more likely scribal error is generally preferable; some noteworthy examples are Imelmann's 'snedeð' in 600 swefeð ond sendeð, Cosijn's 'inwitðanclum' in 749 he onfeng hraðe inwitðancum (78), Klæber's 'secga' in 2252 gesawon seledream (66), Kock's 'ealliren ner' in 2338 eallirenne, and Trautmann's 'behengon' in 3138 ad unwaclicne helmum behongen. These are all convincing by their simplicity when once seen and weighed; it will be observed that all provide good examples of the scribal errors—metathesis, wrong division, similarity of form or the like—illustrated in this chapter.

Many verses in *Beowulf* are metrically short. If the missing word or syllable is unstressed, the context as a rule makes the correction certain, e.g. 947 secg(a) betsta, 1404 (ðær heo) gegnum for, 1546 brad (ond) brunecg (see also 179). Where the word is stressed, alliteration is often a pointer, as in 1889 hægstealda (heap), but not always quite definitely; e.g. in

2139   in ðam sele   Grendeles modor

any one of several alternatives (guðsele, grundsele, gryresele) is a possibility. Occasionally, the poet's usage elsewhere gives us the right word, as in 1329 (æðeling) ærgod, the adjective being the stock epithet in the poem for this noun.

183. The problem is different when we have a number of verses, metrically regular, in which the same word appears to be missing; in these there is no doubt what the word is, but only whether it is correctly omitted. The question we must ask ourselves in this case is whether all or any of the sentences form a syntactical group with its own special idiom. For example, among the noun-clauses in which the conjunction *ðæt* is omitted (34) we found that omission is idiomatic in certain kinds of clause after *cwæð*, but only in these; in all others emendation is necessary, and the emending word is certain. On the other hand, in the sixteen subordinate clauses which omit the pronoun of reference (75) there is no special feature to differentiate them from the 181 regular clauses; all sixteen, therefore, need emendation, and again the emending word (*he* or *heo*) is certain. Three out of the four editions emend them here and there, but none of them in more than four places or on any discoverable principle of choice. The pronoun of reference is frequently omitted in some OE prose texts; it is worthy of note that in the EETS *Orosius* the editor, Sweet, restores it everywhere, sometimes from the second MS., sometimes independently.

184. Let us now consider some cases in which correction is not so simple. A great modern scholar, A. E. Housman, defined textual criticism as 'The *Science* of discovering error in texts and the *Art* of removing it'; by the second part of this definition he meant that emendation, especially in poetry, cannot always be reduced to rule because the poet's art itself cannot be reduced to

rule. In a particular context a good emendation may depend on a right judgement about the poet's idiom or train of thought. Two simple examples will illustrate this. In

849   heorodreore weol
         deadfæge deog:

Sievers' 'deop' is the best of many emendations because *inter alia* it restores a characteristic sentence-parallelism (see 111). On the other hand, in

149   forðam (   ) wearð
         ylda bearnum   undyrne cuð,

where Kl.'s footnote records nine different conjectures, it is strange that they do not include a single example of the equally characteristic appositive to the predicate *cuð* (e.g. gesyne), which seems the most likely of all, cf.

1255   ðæt gesyne wearð,
         widcuð werum.

185. The most troublesome cases of textual error are those in which it is easy to see that something is wrong, but difficult to place one's finger on the spot. Many of these passages are corrupt in two separate places, e.g. 1379 felasinnigne secg (see 178). We have another probable instance in

489   Site nu to symle   ond onsæl meoto
         sigehreð secgum   swa ðin sefa hwette.

It is remarkable that nobody has accepted 'meoto[d]' for the much emended 'meoto'; the context obviously suggests a concluding prayer, with some verb like *sele* in place of 'secgum'. Where then did 'secgum' come from? No doubt from -*mæcgum* just beneath; the scribe, having written the alliterating s- after 'sigehreð', had to refer to his book and, looking at the wrong line, completed the word as 'secgum'. The clause therefore should read 'ond on sæl meotod | sigehreð sele', i.e. 'and may God in due time grant glory even as thy spirit may urge thee'. For the frequent association of *sellan* with God (Metod), see the glossaries; and for the thought and form, cf.

685   ond siððan witig God...
         mærðo deme   swa him gemet ðince.

The metrical type of Sigehreð sele is exactly the same as 67 magodriht micel.

We have a double fault also in

913   He ðær eallum wearð,
     mæg Higelaces,   manna cynne
     freondum gefægra: hine firen onwod.

(1) 'He' must by the rule (41) refer to Heremod in the lines before, but this conflicts with the apposition: the only way out of this dilemma is to remove 'he' and make 'mæg' the grammatical subject; (2) 'freondum' is an absurd appositive to 'eallum manna cynne' and must stand for 'freond' by syntactical attraction to the neighbouring 'cynne', cf. 2392 Eadgilse wearð freond. We now get an idiomatic *ðær*-clause (23) with appropriate sense: 'whereas Beowulf proved himself the kindly friend of all mankind, wickedness overcame Heremod'.

A word must be said about emendation in the longer lacunae of a half line or more (see 177); it will be obvious to the reader that, even when the homoeoteleutic word has some probability, all the rest must be mere guesswork.

186. It should be observed that grammatical correctness is not in itself a guarantee that the MS. reading is sound; there may be a failure in idiom, as in

1888   Com ða to flode   felamodigra
         hægstealda heap,   hringnet bæron....

where idiom demands an infinitive, not a co-ordinate clause, after 'com', and Sievers' 'hringnet beran' (=gongan, as Kl. points out) is therefore better than the MS.; metrically also, 'beran' with its short *e* is preferable after the stressed syllable -*net*: cf. 2754 hringnet beran. This emendation should certainly be admitted to the text. Again in

79   se ðe his wordes geweald   wide hæfde,

we have good grammar but a meaningless construction, viz. the genitive 'wordes' (who had power over his speech=could speak) instead of the dative 'worde' (held sway by his word). This line must be considered in conjunction with

    30   þenden wordum weold   wine Scyldinga,
             leof landfruma,   lange ahte:

where Bright's 'geweald' for 'weold' makes the syntax simple and yields excellent sense: 'while for long he held sway by his words'. The two passages correct each other. A remarkable instance is

    1256   ðætte wrecend ða git
             lifde æfter laðum,   lange ðrage
             æfter guðceare;

The sentence is grammatical, but it is not a helpful comment to say that the words 'lange ðrage', as a description of a single day, are an exaggeration; they are, in fact, nonsense. Since 'æfter guðceare' is not a good apposition to 'æfter laðum', the second 'æfter' would seem to be a mere echo of the first (and perhaps also of 'æfter guðsceare' in 1213); if so, it probably conceals the verb of a clause co-ordinate to 'lifde', e.g. 'iecte', cf. *Jud.* 181 morðra gefremede ond ðæt swyðor gyt ycan wolde. The sense would be appropriate, 'an avenger still lived after the loathly one, [and] added to the long spell of anxious war'.

187. There are passages, besides those we have discussed elsewhere, in which the generally accepted emendation is open to criticism on one ground or another: here are some of them:

    223   Ða wæs sund liden,
             eoletes æt ende

(for 'eoletes' see 173); Thorpe's 'sundlida ealade æt ende' is no doubt substantially right, since 'ðanon' in the next clause implies mention of a ship. The second line, however, with the secondary stress on 'eálàde' is metrically dubious, and the better form would be 'sundlidan ealad æt ende' ('when for the ship the voyage was ended'); a good A type, since in the *nominative* of words like 'Beowulf' 'arfæst' etc. the second syllable may be unstressed.

    367   glædman Hroðgar

If emendation is necessary (and the gloss *hilaris* is hardly appropriate for *glædman* here) the simplest is 'glæd min Hroðgar', cf.

'wine min Hroðgar' and 1181 Ic minne can glædne Hroðulf. The strong 'glæd' is regular, as 1181 shows, where *min* does not immediately precede it (see 90).

431   ðæt ic mote ana   (ond) minra eorla gedryht,
           ðes hearda heap,   Heorot fælsian.

The *gedryht* phrase is regularly preceded by *mid*, which might easily drop out through haplography. The appositive 'ðes hearda heap' includes 'ic'.

747   ræhte ongean
           feond mid folme

'him ræhte ongean' is the simpler emendation, and also provides the sentence with an object.

949   ne bið ðe nænigra gad
           worolde wilna.

This is Grein's correction, adopted by three editors, of the MS. ænigre; it gives us, however, a forbidden trisyllabic anacrusis in this E type; the better emendation is Tr.'s 'ne bid ðe nænges gad', scanning as simple B. The usual scansion of the text as cited is also B, but this ignores the secondary stress on the second syllable of 'nænigra'.

1519   mægenræs forgeaf
           hildebille;   hond (MS. hord) swenge ne ofteah,

The end-position of the negative verb in 1520 (see 52) points to a co-ordinate clause with the same subject as 'forgeaf', and if we write 'hondsweng ne ofteah' we have good sense: '[and] spared not his handstroke'. For the sentence-form we have a close parallel in 2489 feorhsweng ne ofteah, also a co-ordinate clause.

1644   Ða com in gân   ealdor ðegna;

elsewhere the form after 'com' is *gangan*, and there is some evidence that this was the regular infinitive of the verb which had *gæð ga*, etc. as the other moods of the present tense; the MS. form *gan* is a likely haplograph.

1893   gæst[as] grette;

since 'he' in 1900 'he ðæm batwearde sweord...gesealde' other-

wise lacks a noun of reference, Beowulf not having been mentioned,
'gæst gegrette' (cf. 652) is the better correction; the boat-ward
would naturally address the leader.

2297   næs þær ænig mon
        on þære westenne;   hwæðre hilde gefeh,
        beaduweorces hwilum,   on beorh æthwearf:

'wiges', the accepted correction of 'hilde', gives us a sentence
without subject; 'hilde' is a likely misreading of 'he wide', which
would both provide a subject and add the pertinent fact that the
dragon ranged some distance in his search: 'yet be sniffed battle
far and wide at whiles [and] returned to his barrow'. There is no
need to alter 'beaduweorces'.

2384   mærne ðeoden;   him ðæt to mearce wearð

There is no reason to suspect 'mearce' (= country, cf. Weder-
mearce) but something must be wrong with the 3-lift b verse; if
we write 'ðæm hit' in place of 'him ðæt' (metathesis of the two
stems), we get good metre and sense, and restore the sentence-
parallelism to 'ðone selestan etc.' in the two preceding lines:
'the famous prince whose realm it (Sweden) had become'. 'He'
in

2385   He ða for feorme...

like 'hyne' in 2379, now refers to Heardred as it ought to do.

2620   He [ða] frætwe geheold   fela missera

So Sievers, followed by two editors; the temporal adverb, however,
has no point in this sentence, which means 'Hé held the arms for
many a year until his son could achieve earlship'.

3003   ðone ðe ær geheold
        wið hettendum   hord ond rice,
        æfter hæleða hryre,   hwate † Scildingas,
        folcred fremede,   oððe (he) furður gen
        eorlscipe efnde.

A right division of the clauses is important. Note the three time-
words, ær, æfter, oððe; the first clause ends with 'rice' and describes
Beowulf's early manhood, the second refers to his long and bene-
ficent reign which culminates (oððet) in his heroic death: 'who

guarded hoard and realm of old against our enemies [and] after the fall of the princes (Hygelac and Hearded), like the valiant shieldsman he was, advanced his people's good until he achieved heroism yet more (against the dragon)'. The simplest emendation of 3007 *b* is 'hwata scildwiga' in apposition to the subject of the clause; for 'oððe' (=oððæt) see 99.

3038   Ær hi ðær gesegan   syllicran wiht,
        wyrm on wonge,   wiðerræhtes ðær,

There is a double objection to 3038 *a*, (1) the repetition of *ðær* in the same sentence, (2) that *ðær* ought to alliterate over the verb as elsewhere, e.g. in 3008 just above and 3050 just below. The simplest emendation is to remove the first *ðær*; for the sense of the passage see 121, and for the ictus on *ær* 134.

3180   wyruldcyning
        manna mildust   ond monðwærust

Kemble's 'wyruldcyninga' might seem the simplest emendation, but it leaves us with a new difficulty, for the appositive 'manna', so far from being stronger than the first noun, is felt as an anti-climax; 'god' is the usual epithet of praise for a king (cf. god cyning *passim*, 1870 cyning æðelum god, 2563 god guðcyning), and if we write 'wyruldcyning god' here, 'manna mildust' and the other superlatives become proper appositives to 'god'; 'god' might easily have been dropped by a scribe because the sentence seemed complete without it (179).

INDEX OF LINES

in which the text is specially commented on

The numbers on the right refer to sections

SUBJECT INDEX

(Numbers refer to sections)